Backstage Politics

It's nudging sixty years since Phillip Adams' by-line first appeared in an Australian newspaper. As an atheist and contrarian, he's been annoying people ever since. Gough Whitlam calls him 'Australia's most perceptive social critic'. Robert Manne says he's 'perhaps the most remarkable broadcaster in this country's history'. As well as lots of books and TV series, Adams' dozen feature films include *The Adventures of Barry McKenzie* and *Don's Party*. He has chaired many government bodies, won lots of awards, attracted many enemies and remains hyperactive.

Backstage Politics

PHILLIP ADAMS

VIKING
an imprint of
PENGUIN BOOKS

VIKING

Published by the Penguin Group
Penguin Group (Australia)
250 Camberwell Road, Camberwell, Victoria 3124, Australia
(a division of Pearson Australia Group Pty Ltd)
Penguin Group (USA) Inc.
375 Hudson Street, New York, New York 10014, USA
Penguin Group (Canada)
90 Eglinton Avenue East, Suite 700, Toronto, Canada ON M4P 2Y3
(a division of Pearson Penguin Canada Inc.)
Penguin Books Ltd
80 Strand, London WC2R 0RL, England
Penguin Ireland
25 St Stephen's Green, Dublin 2, Ireland
(a division of Penguin Books Ltd)
Penguin Books India Pvt Ltd
11 Community Centre, Panchsheel Park, New Delhi – 110 017, India
Penguin Group (NZ)
67 Apollo Drive, Rosedale, North Shore 0632, New Zealand
(a division of Pearson New Zealand Ltd)
Penguin Books (South Africa) (Pty) Ltd
24 Sturdee Avenue, Rosebank, Johannesburg 2196, South Africa

Penguin Books Ltd, Registered Offices: 80 Strand, London WC2R 0RL, England

First published by Penguin Group (Australia), 2010

1 3 5 7 9 10 8 6 4 2

Cover design by Nikki Townsend © Penguin Group (Australia)
Text design by Karen Scott © Penguin Group (Australia)
Cover illustration by David Follett
Internal illustrations by Bruce Petty
Typeset in 12/17pt Fairfield Light by Post Pre-Press Group, Brisbane, Queensland
Printed and bound in Australia by McPherson's Printing Group, Maryborough, Victoria

National Library of Australia
Cataloguing-in-Publication data:

Adams, Phillip, 1939–
Backstage politics / by Phillip Adams.
9780670073849 (pbk)
Politicians – Australia – Anecdotes
Australia – Politics and government

320.994

penguin.com.au

Introduction

For a dozen years Australia's political opinionista (what Italians call their 'political commentariat') was unevenly divided between the Howard-huggers and the Howard-haters. The huggers dominated, both in number and in volume, with the likes of Andrew Bolt, Janet Albrechtsen, Piers Akerman, Gerard Henderson, Christopher Pearson – and later Noel – forming an anvil chorus of triumphalism. With John Winston firmly in the saddle – and a little later George W. and the neo-cons astride their horses of the apocalypse – the few on what might loosely be called 'the left' felt enfeebled and ridiculed.

Andrew, Janet, Piers, Gerard, Christopher and the rest were waging what they believed to be winning wars in Afghanistan and Iraq, and on history, culture, drugs, refugees, the ABC, the republic, reconciliation and what was left of federal Labor. On the other side? The thin blue line of lines drawn by the Leaks, Pettys and Leunigs (in even the most conservative of papers the cartoonists were permitted to remain bolshie), and the handful of Howard-hating columnists. Tolerated to create the illusion of pluralism.

Through the Howard years, which seemed to stretch beyond eternity, it was Alan Ramsey and I who blazed away at the PM most noisily, me as the 'licensed leftie' at *The Australian* and Alan as the resident grouch at *The Sydney Morning Herald*. While I routinely described Howard as Australia's worst Prime Minister, Alan was more trenchant, calling the PM 'the toad'. My disapproval of Howard was ideological, Ramsey's aesthetic.

So we were not entirely singing the same song. Principal among my problems with Howard was his treatment of refugees, both before, during and after Tampa. Alan, in contrast, was dismissive of asylum-seekers and surprisingly sympathetic to Howard on the 'kids overboard' issue; he felt, for once, that Howard had behaved honestly.

For my own part, I've only ever agreed with Howard on one issue: in finding the notion of retirement repugnant. Having been born just days apart in July 1939, we saw our advancing years as no reason to leave the stage. Yet Alan, a year older, suddenly decided he'd had enough. Not long after Howard's defeat, Alan departed the *Herald*. This provoked a day of national mourning. Well, state-wide mourning; sadly, Alan's writings hadn't been syndicated across this wide brown land. A grand wake in Canberra was attended by many political heavies who had little cause to love him, most notably Paul Keating. (One might suggest that many attended in the spirit of a famous Hollywood funeral for one of the Warner brothers. 'I'm here to make sure he's dead,' said at least one of the mourners.)

A little later I visited the Canberra home Alan shares with the splendid Laura Tingle and interviewed him over cups of tea and Anzac biscuits. Alan had baked the bikkies himself and talked of a 'secret ingredient', ultimately revealed as treacle. But there was nothing treacly about Alan's prose and little in the way of sentimentality in the hour-long chat we subsequently broadcast.

The anecdotes poured out. For example, how and why he'd shouted 'You liar!' at Prime Minister John Gorton from his eyrie in the press gallery. Such yarns were no less fascinating for their familiarity.

But for me there was one surprise. It turned out that Alan's first significant story as an observer of federal politics concerned my first significant involvement with the ALP in the 1960s. Whilst vividly remembering the blazing headlines across the front page of *The Australian*, I'd not noted the by-line. And even if I had, back then the name Alan Ramsey meant little to me – or to anyone else.

So let me begin this book of anecdotes with one that links the careers of two grumpy old men, Ramsey and Adams.

After a few years as a teenage Communist, I'd joined the ALP. I also joined the Fabian Society, which conservative conspiracy theorists have long believed runs Australia – an extraordinary notion, given our inability to raffle ducks in country pubs.

Watching with mounting dread the approach of a federal election that would be fought on the issue of Vietnam, I prepared a secret report for the notorious Victorian Executive of the ALP, a left-wing cabal that preferred ideological purity to the winning of elections. In this they were considerably successful, keeping Labor out of power for yonks. So much so that, down the track, a shiny bright Gough Whitlam would organise a putsch to kick 'em out.

But in 1966 Arthur Calwell was still the leader – facing Harold Holt. As a Fabian, I'd long argued that Australia had effectively had presidential elections since the Menzies era – that people voted for their local candidate as a surrogate for the party leader. Often they'd no idea who the local candidate was – just a name on a how-to-vote card.

Australia's move to presidential-style politics had been intensified by the recent arrival of television. Elections were now being won and lost on the little screen rather than the hustings. In this context, Arthur looked as hapless as Holt looked urbane. Then there was the issue of Vietnam. Holt had nailed Australia's colours to the mast with his notorious 'All the way with LBJ' speech in Washington and, in a display of gratitude, Lyndon Johnson would soon arrive in Australia to cheering (and jeering) crowds – a royal tour more exciting than any of Elizabeth's. The population would be agog at seeing, for the first time in history, a sitting US president sitting on us. LBJ would shamelessly push Holt's barrow in the way that, four decades on, George W. Bush would push John Howard's.

In a presidential contest with Holt, I knew, Calwell was doomed. To prove it, I recorded 'vox pops' with Labor supporters in factories and on footpaths and played them to a shocked and increasingly angry Fabian conference. With my comrades blaming the messenger for the message, I was hissed and booed as we listened to rusted-on Labor supporters ridiculing Calwell on a number of grounds. He dressed poorly – a couple of people complained that he'd been sighted wearing yellow socks with a blue suit. He spoke in a gravelly voice from the corner of his mouth, like a ventriloquist in search of a doll. It was even feared by some Alf Garnettian respondents that Arthur 'wouldn't know which knife and fork to use' when he had lunch with the Queen.

The ALP's view on Vietnam was increasingly being affected by the anti-war movement. One of its most charismatic leaders, Dr Jim Cairns, had his eye on Arthur's job, as did the young Gough Whitlam. Jim and Gough also had their eyes on each other.

My secret report made the startling suggestion that Arthur should be persuaded to leave the country for the duration of the election campaign. With Calwell out of the way, Whitlam and Cairns could work in harness, pushing the ALP line that (a) we would have no part of conscription, and (b) Australian troops would be brought home.

How could Arthur be persuaded to absent himself? My report suggested that he be encouraged to see himself as an 'elder states-man' and wander the world for photo ops with those world leaders who, to a greater or lesser extent, shared our concerns about the Vietnam War. On his meet-and-greet list would be U Thant, the then Secretary-General of the United Nations, His Holiness the Pope, and Madame Gandhi.

To my astonishment, Arthur fell for the flattery. Travelling arrangements were made and he was packing his suitcase. Jim and Gough prepared to tackle Harold and the White House as a double-act. Unfortunately, a copy of the document was leaked to Ken Randall – these days the boss of the National Press Club – who ran a small paragraph on it in *The Australian*. Although few people seemed to notice it, Alan Ramsey saw a major story. Hence the front-page headline the next Saturday morning: 'Secret Report Says Dump Calwell'.

Bugger! My plot instantly unravelled. This unique strategy for a federal election was destroyed. Alan had his first journalistic triumph. And I my first defeat.

(The leak was a large embarrassment to my co-conspirators – the patriotically enchristened Leonard Anzac Reason and Ralph Blunden, both of whom ran advertising agencies with many conservative clients. With McCarthyism lingering in Australia, both Len and Ralph didn't advertise that they were ex-Communists, still employing the techniques they'd picked up as Bolshevik propagandists.)

And so, all those years later, whilst munching Alan's Anzac biscuits – enhanced by treacle – I accused him of winning the election for the Melbourne Club and the White House whilst condemning the ALP to more years in the wilderness. Alan brushed aside the suggestion as he brushed the crumbs off the dining-room table. And he was probably right in saying that Calwell couldn't have won, even had he campaigned from a distant galaxy.

Although my involvements in Australian politics have been tangential, infrequent and often accidental, they've piled up over the years and continue to do so. (Despite being a life-long member of the ALP, I never attended a single branch meeting.) Whilst some of these stories are included in what follows, most are sourced from direct encounters with the personae at their dramatis moments. Many are classics, familiar and mythologised accounts of, for example, Whitlam's self-ridiculing pomposities or Keating's cut and thrust. Others have been contributed by obscure backbenchers or party apparatchiks.

Let the record show that I wrote to every federal politician in the Reps and Senate and the pickings were thin. The most enthusiastic respondent was Barnaby Joyce, who pours out stories as effusively as a ruptured oil well, hinting at the prodigious energies that Tony Abbott finds hard to cap. The overwhelming majority of his colleagues prevaricated, procrastinated or apologised for their inability to recall any event in their political careers that might interest a reader. This goes a considerable distance to explaining why so many of them have managed to have careers in which their anonymity has been protected.

I've also turned to the official literature of Australian

politics – from the memories and memoirs of participants like Mungo MacCallum and Barry Cohen to any number of academic biographers.

So let us honour the efforts of Mungo, Edna Carew, Barry Cohen, Fred Daly, Graham Freudenberg, Paul Kelly, James Killen and other worthy participants or observers of our political fray. I also thank the many readers and listeners who've added to this collection.

In his splendid *Australian Political Anecdotes* (Oxford University Press, 1994), Mungo MacCallum tells of an early sitting of the federal Parliament during its Melbourne incumbency, 'during which a Minister was being heckled mercilessly by a Member of the Opposition'. Eventually the heckler, who was somewhat tired and emotional, gave up and went to sleep in his place. The Minister then walked across the chamber, unbuttoned his fly and urinated in his tormenter's ear.

Hansard, says Mungo, records that 'an incident occurred', but its veracity is as elusive as the mace long missing from the Victorian Parliament. As Mungo points out, it might be 'the ultimate Australian political anecdote: the quintessence of the way the rude colonials adapted the solemnity of the British parliamentary system to suit our own peculiar needs'. This book will return to that theme sixteen years later.

I've limited the book to pretty much what might be described as the modern era, which, in my case, means from the time I've anything that resembles a memory of politics. From late Menzies to the late Rudd.

My first political memory involves the great Menzies, who came, for some inexplicable reason, to Eltham High School. Our headmaster – I'm not sure which one, but we had, in succession, two oddly named incumbents, Mr Moody and Mr Fury – had herded us all into the quadrangle beneath a flagpole engorged with the colonial combo of Southern Cross and Union Jack. But the great man was late to arrive. Very. The tableau in the quad was frozen in time and anxiety.

The mysteriously missing Menzies made it at long last. Imagine our delight when, the next day, we learnt that his chauffeur had got them lost and they'd enquired the location of Eltham High from the local night-cart driver – his truck swilling with excrement and surrounded by its cloud of blowies.

Sadly, many of the best of my best stories, including an intriguing insider's account of the nature of the marriage of John and Janette Howard, cannot be included. Either they are too cruel, too personal or too likely to provoke a libel action. Let Bob Ellis remain pre-eminent in the telling of political anecdotes that provoke litigation.

However, as a special bonus to the readers of this tome, I am willing to tell some of the censored stories, on a strictly personal basis, if and when our paths cross.

Like actors, politicians are great anecdotalists, and to watch a Paul Keating perform them – hilariously – is one of the great joys of life. Neville Wran is even more energetically anecdotal and will range around a room, playing every part. However, for cogent analysis and accurate details I recommend that you read other books – like Freudenberg's history of the Whitlam Government, *A Certain Grandeur*. What follows is probably closer in spirit to the unreliable recollections in Mark Latham's diaries.

Anecdotes are not jokes. When collecting the latter for *The Penguin Book of Australian Jokes*, I'd started with politics. Indeed, the first contribution came from Bob Hawke as Prime Minister. He had sidled up with a leer and said, 'There are two corpses on the

Hume Highway. One's a skittled kangaroo and the other's a politician. What's the difference?' I didn't know. 'There are skid marks before the kangaroo.' Hawke found this infinitely amusing, as did I. And to hear such self-deprecation from the lips of an incumbent Prime Minister said much for Australian irreverence. This is the politics of a country where the pollies don't sit in the back of a limo but up front beside the driver. And where the voters call them by their first name or a diminutive. 'G'day, Bob.' 'G'day, Hawkey.'

Bob's joke seemed quintessentially, defiantly Australian. Emblematic of a nation where not only are tall poppies cut down, but the very tallest poppy can rejoice in the phenomenon. Imagine my disappointment on learning the joke had originated in the United States, where there were skid marks on Route 66 before a dead skunk. Such relocations occurred over and over again with political jokes.

We published a joke about the then Premier of New South Wales, Nick Greiner, taking his Cabinet to lunch and ordering his meal. 'What about the vegetables?' enquires the waiter. Greiner casts a contemptuous eye over his colleagues and says, 'They'll have what I have.' This turned out to derive from an original starring Margaret Thatcher.

Unlike jokes, political anecdotes are specific to the latitude, longitude and chronology of Australian political life. They provide portraits of particular people at particular times.

Paul Keating's frequent and invariably unexpected visits during the Howard years tended to find us both in melancholy mood. But when Paul wasn't intent on giving me lessons in economics, he'd start to tell his yarns. The momentum would pick up and soon I'd be exhausted from laughter.

On top of everything else, Paul is one of the greatest comic talents this country's politics has produced. And with other contenders – from Whitlam to Wran to Mick Young and Bob Collins – he's had some stiff competition. That's what makes politics different from history. Politics is history plus humour. Much of it is R-rated and may contain nudity, sex scenes and even some violence. And almost none of it survives in what passes for 'the record'.

This is not the place to find a solemn, detailed account of the post-Menzies era. But you will be taken backstage to witness politics in the dressing-rooms and from the wings.

Thirty-two years an MP, Fred Daly was both immensely popular and one of Parliament's natural archivists. After thirty years, his *From Curtin to Hawke* is still one of the livelier accounts of federal politics, though he saved the funniest stories for *The Politician Who Laughed*.

Amongst many acute observations, Fred noted that Ministers were rarely appointed to departments that had anything in common with their life experiences, thus making them overly dependent on their Sir Humphreys. Among the examples cited: Ralph Hunt, a Country Party farmer, was Minister for Health. Jim Killen, a one-time jackaroo, was Minister for Defence. Bill McMahon, a lawyer, was Minister for Primary Industry. Hubert Opperman, a professional cyclist, Minister for Immigration.

Warming to his topic, Fred recalled that 'Mr Davidson, an outstanding army officer, was Minister for the Navy; Mr Fred Osborne, a submarine commander in the Second World War, became Minister for Air; and Jack Cramer, a successful real estate agent, was Minister for the Army.'

⁂

Retiring in 1975, Fred Daly liked to tell the story of the new Member who sat next to him in the House. Turning to Fred, he said, 'I like to sit here and look across at the enemy.'

'Son,' said Fred, 'you are looking at the Opposition. The enemy is behind you.'

⁂

Fred recalls Labor legend Pat Kennelly reporting on the funeral of a parliamentary colleague: 'It w-w-w-was a v-v-v-very s-s-s-sad o-c-c-casion h-h-his w-w-w-wife and f-f-f-family w-w-w-were there. There was not a d-d-d-dry eye in the c-c-c-c-cemetery. E-e-everyone w-w-w-was in t-t-t-tears as I w-w-w-watched them f-f-f-file out of the c-c-c-c-cemetery I th-th-thought h-h-how s-s-sad. 300 m-m-mourners with a s-s-s-single th-th-th-thought. Wh-wh-who's g-g-going to w-w-win the pre-s-s-selection?'

⁂

Daly alleges that on the afternoon of the dismissal of the Whitlam Government – 11 November 1975 – an official of the Prime Minister's Department in Canberra phoned Buckingham Palace and asked to speak to the Queen. It was three a.m. when Her Majesty came on the line.

The official said, 'I want to report to Your Majesty that Whitlam is out and Fraser is in.'

The Queen replied, 'Why ring me at this hour of the morning to tell me the cricket score?'

Vince Gair, former Premier of Queensland and Leader of the Democratic Labor Party in the Senate, was an easy target for the satirist. I recall once describing him as 'a Halloween pumpkin wherein the candle of intelligence flickers but fitfully'.

But he was pretty good at insults himself. He famously observed of Sir Billy Snedden that 'he wouldn't make an impression on a bloody soft cushion and wouldn't go two rounds with a revolving door'.

Daly recalls Whitlam as having a 'well ordered mind as he always sacked or changed his ministers in alphabetical order'. Fred cited Bryant, Cameron, Crean, Cairns and Connor. 'Sir John Kerr also liked the system,' Fred added, 'but threw a spanner in the works by starting from the other end of the alphabet.'

W. C. 'Billy' Wentworth, the legendary New South Wales Liberal, wrote a poem on 'the gag', a parliamentary ploy to discourage debate:

Should an Opposition Member try to fan the sinful ember?
A resistance to the Party that has got you in its bag

You may stifle protestation, and prevent expostulation,
By the simple application of the Gag.

There are ways and ways of dealing with a man of hostile feeling
You may rule him with road metal, you may settle him with slag
You may whip him with a wattle, or may bruise him with a bottle
But the surest way to throttle him is the Gag.

Anticipating George W. Bush's maladroit use of the English language, Kep Enderby, once Minister for Manufacturing Industry, educated the Parliament with the revelation that 'most of our imports come from overseas'.

In *A Thinking Reed*, Barry Jones tells a great story about Herbert 'Doc' Evatt, the most divisive Labor leader prior to Mark Latham. Barry, an Evatt protégé, persuaded the great man to open his foredoomed campaign for the safe Liberal seat of Camberwell, for which my oldest friend had been endorsed 'essentially because nobody else wanted it'. The election was occurring while the Labor split was splitting, so it was decided to employ such patriotic props as the Queen, the anthem and the flag. The table on stage was covered in purple cloth, behind which were a Union Jack and a framed colour photo of Her Majesty mounted on her horse, Winston. One of Jones' activists, Norm Griffiths, had brought his gramophone and intended to play his very own seventy-eight of *God Save the Queen*.

No sooner had Evatt established himself majestically on stage than Norm applied needle to groove. At the sound of the drum roll, all stood to endure an orchestral rendition of the anthem – and then sat down. But this was premature. There was more. Norm's gramophone produced sounds of a chorus singing the first verse. Everyone stood up again.

God save our gracious Queen,
Long live our noble Queen,
God save the Queen!
Send her victorious,
Happy and glorious,
Long to reign over us:
God save the Queen!

Whereupon everyone sat down again. Whereupon Norm's gramophone provided the second verse.

Thy gracious gifts in store,
On her be pleased to pour;
Long may she reign!
May she defend our laws,
And ever give us cause
To sing with heart and voice
God save the Queen!

'For the third time the crowd sat,' Barry recalls, but they hadn't reckoned with Norm or the full three-verse version orchestrated by Sir Edward Elgar. Everyone struggled erect for . . .

Oh Lord, our God, arise,
Scatter her enemies,
And make them fall!
Confound their politics,
Frustrate their knavish tricks,
On thee our hopes we fix,
God save us all!

As the audience sat for the fourth time, Evatt glared at his protégé. 'His face was suffused with rage. He hissed: "You only did this to make a fool of me. Calwell put you up to it!"'

This traumatic memory may help to explain Barry's commitment to republicanism.

In *Inside Australian Politics*, Jim Killen tells of Arthur Calwell picking up an honour after an election defeat. Arthur advised Jim on protocol, should he, like Arthur, ever be admitted to the membership of the Privy Council. 'Look, if you're ever appointed, remember you do *not* turn your back on the sovereign. You walk backwards to your place.'

Jim asked how that might be managed. Arthur said he'd 'picked out a seam in the carpet'.

Perhaps using the same technique, Jim recalls 'Bill McMahon also performing very well', and adds the thought: 'Who would have thought it possible for Billy McMahon to walk backwards in a straight line?'

Or, for that matter, for someone so devious to walk in any direction in a straight line.

When LBJ was campaigning blatantly for Holt – a pre-echo of George W.'s endorsement of John Howard as 'the man of steel' – he told the Australian PM to 'make any arrangements you like for me – I'll even kiss the mothers and nurse the babies. You work out the details, I'll do the rest.'

LBJ was as good as his word and was equally pliant in the company of Liberal Premiers. When driving through jeering crowds in Sydney, the over-excited New South Wales Premier, Robert Askin, shouted, 'Run over the bastards!'

In 1968 Gough Whitlam nosily resigned from the leadership of the ALP, which he'd only recently acquired. The hissy fit infuriated many of us who'd supported Gough in his struggles to succeed the lachrymose Arthur Calwell.

Jim Cairns, the icon of the left, decided to run against Whitlam for the leadership – for a second time. Laid low by a virus, Jim would emerge from his bedroom to conduct press conferences on the verandah of his Hawthorn home – dressed in his 'jamas and dressing gown. Not a good look. Jim also penned a letter to all members of Caucus, asking for their support. But before he sent it I was asked to do a rewrite.

Sitting on Jim's counterpane, I made the text far less respectful. Where Jim repeatedly talked about 'Mr Whitlam', I insisted on a curt 'Whitlam'. The 'Misters' were symptomatic of Jim's approach – the entire letter seemed excessively polite. In roughing it up, I added a question: 'Whose party is this – ours or his?'

Decades later, Whitlam's speechwriter and amanuensis Graham Freudenberg described my words as 'amongst the most powerful in Labor history'. Clearly so, as to everyone's astonishment (especially Jim's and mine) Cairns came within a couple of votes of ousting Whitlam. Gough was that close to crashing rather than crashing through. Resentment over Gough's hauteur almost ended his career before it began.

Jenny Hocking tells the story in *Gough Whitlam: A Moment in History*: 'Cairns encapsulated the core of the discord in the single memorable question, "Whose party is this, ours or his?"' It was dramatic, precise and extraordinarily effective.

Jenny reminds us that had three people changed their minds, Gough would have been a goner. Two mind-changes would have been humiliating, one or two might have proved fatal. They would certainly have cost him any claim to a mandate. But though the vote was neither as deep as a well nor as wide as a church door, it sufficed. As Senator Kennelly would say, 'You can keep all the logic, brother, give me the numbers.'

What wasn't understood – either by Whitlam at the time or by Gerard Henderson in a recent column – is that neither Jim nor I wanted to win. Jim knew he was perceived as too radical to lead the party to victory, most of all in those turbulent Cold War years with Vietnam raging. Our purpose was simply to give Gough a kick in the backside.

It was so painful a kick that Gough took years to forgive me (if he ever entirely did), always drawing himself to his full height and snarling down at me, 'Jim Cairns' campaign manager!'

Though he would later serve as Gough's Treasurer and Deputy Prime Minister, personally Jim was cast into the outer darkness, where he'd remain. He told me that because of Gough's near-death experience in the Caucus vote, he never spoke directly to Jim again.

Just before the Vietnam election, Jim and I were asked to address a gathering of candidates. They were piled high in a university lecture room and expected Jim to read them the riot act on Vietnam – about the need for the immediate withdrawal of Australia troops.

But what Jim had to say first surprised and then angered. At the end they booed him! And why? Because he refused to employ the over-simplified, slogan-chanting approach to the war appropriate to moratorium marches. Jim explained his opposition to complete withdrawal – he believed that some Australian soldiers would need to remain in Hanoi to form a protective enclave. The South Vietnamese would need to be shielded from vengeance. 'If not, there could well be a mass slaughter of people the Viet Cong regard as collaborators,' Jim said.

That's how I remember Jim in the years before Junie – before his long-suppressed sexuality blossomed into a sort of counter-cultural ecstasy and he became a disciple of Wilhelm Reich and his 'orgone box'. Jim was much more thoughtful and calibrated in his views than either his critics or his supporters.

During the Vietnam War, ASIO was hyperactive – on the trail of anyone who could be remotely considered a subversive. Having joined the Communist Party the year after being expelled from the Boy Scouts, I was amongst their targets. The National Archives once let me glimpse my ASIO file, something the organisation had for decades denied having. Despite its extensive blackings-out, it revealed that ASIO had opened my dossier just after I turned sixteen.

But probably the thickest file of all belonged to Jim Cairns. The likes of Jim and I got used to hearing clicks on the phone and, from time to time, finding someone crouching in the shrubbery under a window.

Jim had good reason to believe that his inner circle had been penetrated and that quite a few 'friends' were ASIO spies. And when we'd gather at Jim and Gwen's, in leafy Hawthorn, he'd take the trusted ones aside and warn us that there were a couple of spooks at the gathering taking part in our strategic discussions on anti-Vietnam tactics. Just as the FBI's plants represented a majority of members of the United States' Communist Party, the lads from ASIO were often in the majority at our meetings and probably reported on each other. But Jim refused to close the front door, let alone lock it. The Cairns always kept an open house. In 1969, he paid the price when a couple of thugs wandered in and bashed both Jim and Gwen – Jim seriously.

I visited Jim whilst he was recuperating, and he told me that the invaders had come straight to the house after bashing the doorman at a local RSL 'with a statue of Simpson and his donkey'. Many of us believed that Jim never fully recovered from the attack, and that his head injuries played a part in his subsequent embrace of Reich's sexual theories. But our JC, like a famous predecessor with the same initials, refused to hold a grudge and publicly forgave his assailants. The bashing didn't stop him, as chair of the Vietnam moratorium, leading around 100 000 people in the largest political protest Australia had ever seen.

Junie Morosi was Jim's muse – a relationship that was condemned, under parliamentary privilege, by a newly elected MP. It was John Howard who drew public attention to a relationship that was scarcely a state secret. Indeed, Cairns didn't seek to repudiate his relationship with Junie, once publicly proclaiming 'a kind of love' for her. Nonetheless, he did become somewhat Clintonian ('I did not have sexual relations with that woman') when, in 1982, he initiated a defamation case before the Supreme Court of New South Wales in which he denied, on oath, a sexual affair with her. By the end of his life he had admitted to perjury. And, as will be revealed later, Gough Whitlam was in possession of some of the evidence.

When Jim's political career was destroyed, he became an energetic proselytiser of the countercultural lifestyle, with particular emphasis on the erotic. He was ridiculed for selling his self-improvement books from a card table he'd erect at suburban markets. But our regular conversations – we talked for the rest of his life – confirmed him as amongst the most fascinating and complex characters in the history of the ALP. Little surprise that his funeral in October 2003 (Jim died of bronchial pneumonia at the age of eighty-nine) was almost as big as a moratorium march.

In the early 1960s the poisoned chalice of the Victorian Labor leadership fell to Clive Stoneham, a dull and decent man, plump as a Parliament House pigeon, who was doomed in his attempts to defeat the rat-cunning Henry Bolte. I was a 23-year-old who divided his time between left-wing politics and the furnace hold of capitalism as a young advertising executive.

I was sitting in my St Kilda Road office – which doubled as a storeroom – when Stoneham, whom I'd never met, phoned. 'I want you to come in and see me,' he said.

'What about?'

'I'll tell you when you get here.'

'Where's here?'

'My office in Parliament House. You climb up the front steps, go in the door on the left and ask someone. But please come soon – I really need your help.'

There was something poignant, even desperate, in the tone of his voice so I caught a tram in to Bourke Street and another up the hill. I then trudged up the stairs – worthy of the Odessa Steps sequence in Eisenstein's *Battleship Potemkin* – and followed orders by pushing open the giant door on the left.

Blinking in the gloom, I found myself being interrogated by a man in uniform. 'I'm here to see the Opposition Leader,' I said.

I was shown into a vast chamber that dwarfed Stoneham both physically and psychologically. The tiny figure behind the great desk couldn't have looked lonelier or more lost.

I suddenly recalled a BBC comedy sketch I'd seen a few days earlier, in which an ordinary suburbanite answered a knock on the door to be confronted by someone from Buckingham Palace saying, 'The Queen wants you to form a government.'

For Stoneham said, 'I want you to write my policy speech.'

'But I've never written a policy speech.'

'Neither have I, but they think I have. I told them I'd written it already.'

I sat opposite the Leader of Her Majesty's Opposition and continued feebly protesting. He'd have none of it.

'Look, I really need your help.'

'Well, a policy speech is about policy. Do you have any?'

'Yeah, I've got a few here somewhere.' And he shoved a pile of documents towards me. 'But if you can think of some yourself, just write them in.'

And, Scout's honour, that's what I did. I wrote the Opposition

Leader's policy speech, liberally enriching it with ideas of my own. Needless to say, we lost the election.

In the June 1969 Victorian elections, Allan Fraser, a federal MP from New South Wales, was recruited as campaign director. The campaign was to be launched by Opposition Leader Clive Stoneham in the Prahran Town Hall and would be broadcast live on television.

On this occasion, Clive was not using one of my speeches but something prepared by the ALP's head office. The idea was that Clive would read the speech from large cue cards. At the top of the first card his own name had been written in big capitals: 'CLIVE'. But the calligraphy proved somewhat confusing.

When the telecast began, Fraser was standing by the first card pointing at 'CLIVE'. Stoneham was unresponsive, so Fraser tapped the name again and again.

The penny dropped and Clive began his election speech with, 'Thank you, Olive.'

My involvement with Victorian politics – with Premiers past, present and potential – continued for many years after my brief stint as a policy speechwriter for Clive Stoneham. But my strongest friendship was – and remains – with John Cain, who became an immensely popular Premier following his defeat of the Liberals in April 1982.

A Keynesian strongly opposed to the doctrines of economic

rationalism, Cain's was the first Labor Government in Victoria for twenty-seven years – and I found myself a member of the team working on his second election campaign.

While others wrote the policy speech, I helped plot the campaign launch. It was to take place at the Channel 0 studios (these days Channel Ten), established by Sir Reginald Ansett, a considerable distance from the city.

We couldn't hope to replicate the 'It's Time' feeling that Gough had employed in 1972, when every known celebrity was anxious to chorus the anthem in what was a purely presidential campaign. But we did manage to get a few soapie stars to add a hint of glamour to the presence of such federal luminaries as Bill Hayden. We hired the only stretch limo in Melbourne and kept our celebs hidden behind the studio; they took it in turns to be driven to the front of the studios before entering the building. In the era before digital cloning – nowadays a dozen extras can be turned into 10000 and one prop boat into an armada – the effect was of not one but a succession of stretch limos delivering the high, the mighty and the familiar to a truly grand event.

Our glamorous guests duly waved at the cameras and then took their places in the auditorium, then John mounted the podium and began to read his speech.

Just a few minutes into his performance there was a calamity – all the lights went out. A complete power failure to the entire channel and, as it turned out, the surrounding district.

As John faded to black, along with the audience and the telecast, I was convinced we were the victims of political sabotage – if not a terrorist attack. After an eternity, the standby generators kicked in and we had to do the whole thing again. Including the circling of the limo. Thoroughly unnerved by the happenings, the Premier was less persuasive, the audience less exuberant. It turned out that the problem was a possum that had entered the electrical system and toasted itself on some critical writing. Stirring the possum.

Gary Humphries, Senator for the ACT, recalls a rumour that MLA Dennis Stevenson used to sleep in his suite in the Assembly building.

'One evening as the Assembly debated into the night some important matter, I was on my feet delivering a passionate speech when suddenly the lights of the chamber went out and the building was plunged into darkness – a power failure! There were a few moments of stunned silence before, out of the darkness, one MLA quipped, "Dennis's electric blanket must have shorted."'

On the occasion of the next Victorian state election, in 1985, I joined forces with Peter Faiman. Destined to direct *Crocodile Dundee* and the opening ceremony of the Sydney Olympics, he came up with a very different approach. We persuaded John to dump the usual hall full of Labor faithful and to launch his campaign as a surprise attack – in the form of a press conference.

The Premier was in the habit of strolling from his office down a long corridor into a room full of print and television journalists, where he'd make a statement and answer questions. Little did the press know that, on this occasion, they'd be on camera too – Peter's cameras.

Our crew followed John from his desk, out the door and down

the hall. He took his usual place at the lectern and then, to everyone's astonishment, announced his campaign and rattled through his policies. The press became extras, hostages to an exercise in postmodernism. Instead of an 'It's Time' chorus and a balloon drop, it looked like a backstage documentary. It might have made a good episode for *The West Wing*.

But, like Queen Victoria, the Victorian media were not amused. And it probably wasn't a great idea to get them offside at the outset.

John Cain was an almost Calvinist Premier. For reason of realpolitik I'd urge him to have social intercourse with Collins Street. Not full carnal relations like Bob Hawke or Brian Burke, but at least the ability to talk about legitimate relationships between business and state government. But, like a previous JC, John's inclination was to chase the moneylenders from the temple. He may, indeed, have had vestigial ideas about socialism. Certainly he refused to accept anything that might be seen as compromising his political integrity. He was a Premier who declined free tickets to opening nights of the opera, ballet or theatre, though his reluctance to attend such events may have had other motives. If he wanted to see something he would insist on buying tickets. He wouldn't permit a staff-member to get them on his behalf. Resolutely democratic, he'd stand in a queue.

John's disinterest in the arts certainly disqualified him from serious contention as their Minister. But, on the André Malraux principle, I urged him to keep the arts within his department; it would make life easier for me, as I was soon to be anointed President of the Victorian Council for the Arts.

On the day John announced his ministry, I saw that he'd ignored my suggestion. He had no ambitions to be a Medici princeling. So I searched the allocation of portfolios, up and down the list of names, but found no mention of the Arts. Not anywhere. It seemed he'd forgotten all about them. When I pointed this out, there was a last-minute flurry and, lo and behold, Race Mathews, who was Minister for things like the Police and Racing, copped them.

This was no bad thing; Race was a man of culture. He had, after all, served as Gough's aide-de-camp prior to 1972 and had breathed life into the Victorian Fabians before becoming a state MP.

The great thing about the Arts portfolio is that it gives infinite possibilities for photo ops. With divas, film stars, dancers, artists and maestros. And you get invited to all sorts of grand events.

One of these was the Italian earthquake concert at the recently opened cultural complex on the banks of the Yarra. A cadenza of concert halls, of which the biggest had been booked for one of those hastily organised fundraisers. With Italian villages in ruins, and a large local Italian community, there were plenty of volunteers to perform and give speeches. It was a bit like Noah's ark, with artistes entering two by two. Two ballet dancers, two opera singers, two actors giving poetry readings – and various orchestral permutations.

But it has to be admitted that people attended the event as an act of duty. Most would have preferred to be a few kilometres away at the Hilton Hotel, where the Logies were being staged. Where small statuettes shaped like suppositories were being presented (it always seemed to me that it would have been more appropriate to insert them). But despite the ugliness of the Logies – for some reason, almost all arts awards are hideous in appearance – it was the more glamorous of the gala events that evening.

I was the compere of the earthquake concert and did my best to convince the audience that they were having a marvellous evening. But if they were indifferent to the entertainment, they were increasingly resentful of the speeches. And waiting in the wings was Race Mathews, who was to give the major address of the evening.

I went on stage and adlibbed the following story. 'Unfortunately, the Minister for the Arts, Race Mathews, cannot be with us tonight. He is attending the Logies at the Hilton.' (At this point you could feel the suppressed rage in the stalls.) 'However, I have been fortunate enough to engage the services of that great local comic, Campbell McComas.

'As you know, ladies and gentlemen, Campbell makes a living by fooling attendees at conferences into believing he's a professor from Harvard or a professional golf player from Arkansas. They sit there listening solemnly to the performance and only realise they've been gulled at its end. But on this occasion, Campbell has agreed to impersonate Race Mathews and to give the sort of speech the Minister would have given had he been here. Rather than at the Logies.'

Race heard nothing of this. What he did hear was tumultuous applause when he walked onto the stage. For perhaps the first and last time in his life, he was clapped, cheered and given the sort of reception that politicians dream of.

It has to be said that, over his years in politics, Race had become somewhat pompous. Much of his public persona echoed that of his erstwhile employer, Gough Whitlam, all the more so because they shared a similar physicality.

Even Gough would have been thrilled at this reception. Race left the stage to something just short of a standing ovation. And he would only learn the truth of what happened the following day.

❦

When the burghers of nineteenth-century Victoria decided to build a grand Government House, business was booming. So they decided to make it very grand indeed. HM Queen Victoria was not amused that their dining room would be more splendid than hers at Windsor. She made her views clear but the Victorians ignored them. What they created above the Yarra, now standing between the Botanic Gardens and the Shrine of Remembrance, was a splendid, neo-classical pile that has always been impeccably maintained. Lots of white paint.

For generations the place was used to park minor royals or British generals or both. More than your fair average quality, the appointees were welcomed with palpitating excitement by Victoria's bunyip aristocracy, particularly those who were members of the Melbourne Club.

We could fill a book with anecdotes about the nation's most influential club, perched near the top of Collins Street, where even Sir Robert Menzies was effectively blackballed. As were, in due course, the brothers Myer, Kenneth and Baillieu. Some mysteries remain about the reasons Menzies was denied admission – there were rumours he'd had an affair with the wife of a prominent Sydney publisher – but there was no doubt as to why the Myers were unacceptable. Jews.

Two of the GGs sent to Victoria from GB before the ALP changed the policy (leading to the likes of Winneke, Murray, McCaughey, McGarvie, Gobbo and Landy) were knighted Poms; as such, they were warmly welcomed by club members. One was General Sir Reginald Alexander Dallas Brooks GCMG, KCB, KCVO, DSO, KStJ, and the other was his military colleague Major General Sir Rohan Delacombe KCMG, KBE, CB, DSO, KStJ.

Dallas Brooks couldn't have fitted the role more perfectly had he been signed by Central Casting. Which, in effect, he was. Yet a scandal, never fully reported, lay ahead. Apparently unhappy with both the quantity and quality of paintings around the place, he'd phoned the oddly named National Gallery of Victoria and requested extra canvases. Imagine everyone's embarrassment at the end of his term when it was discovered that he'd taken them back to England. When polite inquiries were conducted, Brooks said he'd assumed they were gifts.

Sir Rohan Delacombe, affectionately known as Jumbo, had been in charge of Spandau Prison, where Rudolf Hess had been incarcerated, and had apparently behaved a bit like Captain Queeg in *The Caine Mutiny*. It seems he was forever initiating courts martial about little issues like missing strawberries. So Jumbo had to be relocated and, lo and behold, Victoria had a vacancy.

So in 1963 Jumbo Delacombe arrived in town, moved into the wedding cake on the hill and became quite popular. It was hard to believe that this amiable duffer had ever been grumpy in his life.

At this time, there were two places where I was never invited: the Melbourne Club and Government House. But I became quite friendly with an aide-de-camp who would retain his vice-regal employment for decades. And he offered to sneak me in a side door for a guided tour.

I saw the offending dining room and the other state rooms but was then taken back stage. Here was where Queen Elizabeth had stayed and here is Queen Elizabeth's personal toilet. With a beautifully varnished seat. (Legend has it that toilet seats were always freshly varnished whenever a royal visit was anticipated.) I was encouraged to sit on it and feel the vibes.

Then we entered the Governor's private rooms and I was given a peek at his bedroom. Now, what I'm about to tell you is so extraordinary that you will believe that I'm being satirical, or at least hyperbolic. Not so. Jumbo Delacombe's bedroom was full, from floor to ceiling, with bobbing balloons. A remarkable menagerie of inflated animals, of every possible hue.

Given his nickname, I looked around for a jumbo. At that very moment the aide-de-camp emitted a strangled cry. 'Oh my God! His elephant is puckered!' And he rushed across to the deflating creature and provided mouth-to-valve resuscitation.

Others might have been deflated by the remote posting to the colonies but Delacombe served Victoria well. He had to endure, for example, the 1966 visit of Lyndon Baines Johnson and his thuggish security men. One morning, while the President was in residence, Jumbo left the building and went for a walk in the grounds, as was his custom. Imagine his astonishment when, on his return to the front door, he was refused entry. His splutters of outrage fell on deaf ears.

As did his aide-de-camp's complaint about the behaviour of those protecting the President. Of whom the worst was the bloke who ran beside the President's limo on public occasions. Named Rufus Youngblood, he was a formidable figure and, it seemed, spent much of the night standing to attention whilst his president slept. To the horror of his hosts, he smoked cigars and ground the butts into the Governor's very posh carpet.

I forgot to ask whether LBJ's buttocks had also graced the Queen's toilet seat. If so, imagine what that wooden halo would fetch were it to be sold at Sotheby's or on eBay.

In 1969, three years after JFK's assassination and coinciding with Ted Kennedy's adventure at Chappaquiddick, Barry Jones invited Malcolm Muggeridge to Australia for a lecture tour. Barry and I welcomed Malcolm at the old Essendon Airport, where he emerged from a very long flight as bright as a button. Having only seen him on black-and-white television, I was astonished to discover that the editor of *Punch* – who eerily resembled Mr Punch – was as red as a boiled lobster. Far from being exhausted by the trip, Malcolm proceeded to talk pretty much all night, with a heavy emphasis on stories about the sexual proclivities of the famous.

Previously priapic, Malcolm had become a passionate Christian and would soon turn Mother Teresa, by no means a beauty, into a spiritual pin-up. Though he would clearly see Teresa's inner beauty in due course, he was blind to Yoko Ono's, describing her almost gleefully as 'the ugliest woman on earth'.

Then it was on to Jack Kennedy, whom both Jones and Adams viewed with considerable admiration. Malcolm talked of JFK as being the most sexually rapacious politician since Mussolini; like the Italian dictator, he made a habit of 'fornicating with women on his desk'. This was news to us and we were thin-lipped at the revelations. Decades before Bill and Monica, Jack was bonking furiously in the Oval Office, not merely in the stationery cabinet.

We're talking of a time when such activities were rarely reported. Before, for example, the affairs of a Cairns or a Hawke were grist to the media mill. And at this late stage, one can but wonder which Australian politician might yet claim a place in *The Guinness Book of Records*. Hawkey? My money would be on a past and still living leader of the National Party, whose sexual athleticism, in the old Parliament House, remains legendary. Or should the laurels go to a more recent Victorian Premier, whose embrace of parliamentary staff made Mike Rann seem a celibate?

NASA confirms that Barry Jones' brain is visible from outer space. This is not surprising, as that's where it came from.

When *60 Minutes* was doing a story on my friend, I revealed that not one but two babies from the planet Krypton were sent to earth in rocket-powered cribs. One grew up to become Clark Kent, a journalist at the *Daily Planet*. The other became a schoolteacher, lawyer, Victorian MP and, ultimately, a federal Minister.

Picking up on my revelations, *60 Minutes* depicted Barry emerging from Parliament House to the theme from the *Superman* movie and it fitted him like a glove.

(Incidentally, one must recall what doomed Krypton. It was all the fault of the intergalactic warlord Mad Minchen, who, denying there were CO_2 problems, allowed the previously pretty planet to develop runaway climate change.)

Barry's brain, faster than a speeding bullet and capable of leaping very tall problems, was not particularly attuned to day-to-day problems. Let me demonstrate with my fondest BOJ anecdote.

He visited the farm, and the party president and I climbed into a four-wheel drive to tour our wild and magnificent landscape. Not that Barry is particularly interested in landscape, as such. Unless feet, in ancient times, had walked upon the pastures green, leaving behind them either circles of megaliths or ruined cathedrals. But he was doing his best to feign enthusiasm.

When we arrived at the first gate I explained a rural tradition. Whoever is sitting in the front seat by the driver is expected to hop out and open the gate, closing it after the passage of the vehicle so as to constrain the cattle. Barry clambered out to fulfil this obligation and found it more difficult than you might expect for someone with an IQ the size of an IBM mainframe. It was, let me assure you, the simplest of gates to open. No chains to disentangle, no snap-locks to part. Just a loop, which quoit-like encircled the post. It was a gate that even a cow could open with its moist nose. Barry, however, tugged and pulled at it for some time without solving the problem. I shouted encouragement at first, then mild criticisms. Finally he managed it, swung the gate open and I drove through.

In the rear-vision mirror I then watched him trying to reverse the procedure with wire and post. When he finally managed it, I called out, 'Barry, we have a problem.'

He looked at me, somewhat puzzled.

'You're on the wrong bloody side!'

I remembered that story a few years later when I was filming *The Big Questions* with Professor Paul Davies, who may well be another extraterrestrial. I'd opted to shoot the series on science – everything from quantum mechanics to cosmology – in a stretch of desert beyond Coober Pedy, and the producers had decided to fit Paul out in R. M. Williams gear. Which, on Paul, who closely resembles the sort of C of E vicar you might see in an episode of *Midsomer Murders*, looked decidedly bizarre.

Paul is very proud of his intellect. On a previous occasion he told me, with a mixture of sadness and vanity, that 'perhaps three people on earth know what I'm talking about'. Despite our frequent collaborations on both radio and stage, it was clear I wasn't one of them.

Paul chuckled at Barry's problem whilst, at the same time, trying to do up the R. M. Williams belt that went with his R. M. Williams trousers. It was one of those numbers with two loops that requires a snake-like manoeuvre. After two or three goes, Paul looked as hapless as Barry had with the gate. It made me feel a glow of pleasure. I may not be one of the three who understands Paul Davies but at least I can put on my own trousers.

After Harold Holt disappeared in the turbulent waters off Portsea on 17 December 1967, there'd been an unseemly scramble to succeed him. Don Chipp told John Larkin of 'two well-known Liberals in particular who'd been very close to Holt who needed to be actually comforted, one of whom was near hysteria. He was crying, declaring his love for Harold Holt and stating he would never recover from his grief.'

Yet a few hours later things were different. Chipp, a very junior Minister (number twenty-five in a pecking order of twenty-seven) was asked to appear on the seven p.m. news to pay a tribute. 'I said that surely there would be more senior Ministers or officials who would be available, but I was wrong . . . the grab for the coveted prize of Prime Minister had already begun . . . The numbers men, the powerbrokers, had put the word out that Harold Holt had been on a downer and it was not advisable to be associated with him, even though he was dead.' HSV7 found no one else willing to appear.

The list of people unavailable, Chipp recalled, included 'the telephone sniveller of the early afternoon . . . What a bastard of a thing to do.'

Don Chipp and I became friends when he was Minister for Customs in 1970 – and fighting the good fight against Australia's insane censorship laws. He liked to tell the story about a time when one out of every two *Playboys* was banned. According to Don, no magazine was permitted to enter Australia if it contained photographs revealing pubic hair – and one senior official took his job so seriously that he examined centrefolds with a magnifying glass. Don also enjoyed the story of a customs officer removing a book from the luggage of a returning citizen because of its title, *Fun in Bed*. It was a book of distractions and amusements for sick children.

S ince the dawn of time, Liberal leaders had been chosen at the Melbourne Club, an organisation of such impeccably conservative credentials that it denied membership even to Robert Menzies. Like cardinals meeting in the Sistine, members of the club would cogitate upon contenders and, in due course, emit a puff of white smoke out into Collins Street. But this practice came to a sudden end with the election of a dark horse – John Gorton – to the Liberal leadership. The Melbourne Club's thoroughbred candidate, Paul Hasluck, was an early scratching.

In one of the quirks of Australian politics, Barry Jones played a consequential part in Gorton's unexpected ascendency. As a schoolteacher, Jones had had dealings with Gorton when he was the Minister for Education. Although he was then still a rank outsider in the race to the Lodge, Barry had invited Gorton to appear on his pioneer talkback radio program as well as an interview program that he presented on Channel Seven.

Gorton's performances were creditable and gave his candidacy some momentum – and he rewarded Barry by inviting him to stay at the Lodge soon after he'd moved in. While Bettina was having cocoa in the kitchen, Barry and the new PM sat by an open fire and discussed the future. Gorton muttered, 'I don't know what to do about Canada. I've never really liked Canadians.'

Barry pointed out that 'things are different in Canada now'. In response to Gorton's puzzlement, Barry said, 'You know, Trudeau.'

There was silence, then Gorton said, 'Okay, what's a Trudeau?'

'He's the new Prime Minister!'

'What happened to Lester Pearson?'

'Gone,' said Barry.

'Bugger me,' said Gorton. And then he remembered something. 'But now that you mention it, I remember signing a telegram that Tony Eggleton brought in.'

Gorton's affection for Barry enabled us to recruit him to the cause of an Australian film industry. John sent Barry, Peter Coleman and me on a quick jaunt around the planet to come up with ideas to revive the industry. Peter, who was briefly an editor of *The Bulletin* and would be, more briefly, the Leader of the Opposition in New South Wales – he is now fully employed as the father-in-law of Peter Costello and the co-author of his autobiography – wasn't getting on very well with Barry. Soon the both of them were in a major sulk.

Like Whitlam with Cairns, they wouldn't talk to each other directly, so I was kept busy go-betweening. With the three of us squeezed into the back of an official car, Barry would say, 'Tell Coleman such-and-such,' and Coleman would say, 'Tell Barry such-and-such.' It went on for weeks and was particularly difficult at ambassadorial cocktail parties.

In due course, Peter left the delegation – but not entirely because of the tension between himself and Barry Owen Jones. As I wrote at the time, he had decided to avoid the Soviets and Eastern Europe because he thought 'Communism might be catching'.

Not long after John Gorton became Prime Minister he had to make an official visit to South-East Asia, where he conducted a press conference. Things weren't going too well and got even worse when a journalist from a major Asian paper stood and asked the following question: 'Prime Minister, what do you think of the general SEATO policy?'

Gorton stared at his interrogator blankly, then turned to an aide and asked – in a whisper that everyone could hear – 'Who the fuck is General Seato?'

Having left Peter Coleman on the other side of the Iron Curtin, Barry and I proceeded to Moscow, where we were welcomed by *Pravda* (somewhere in the files there's a photograph of the two of us tossing snowballs at each other outside the Kremlin) and by Sir Frederick Blakeney, the Australian Ambassador. Our embassy was a splendid nineteenth-century building created for a favourite mistress by a wealthy industrialist and friend of the Tsar. Sir Fred proudly showed us a particularly magnificent fireplace where, he told us, the great baritone Cherkasov had frequently sung melancholy dirges about the Volga. The room also had a magnificent chandelier which was sadly dulled by dust. The embarrassed ambassador told us that Foreign Affairs had refused to advance him the funds necessary to clean it.

But Fred's biggest problem was that he kept dusting off memories of 'the Doc'. He told us of recurring nightmares in which, suddenly, Evatt would come thundering into a room and loudly bully him. Decades after the Doc's death, Sir Fred still lived in dread of him.

He apologised that the Embassy couldn't help out with an interpreter and warned us that the one the Soviets would supply would almost certainly be a KGB agent.

He turned out to be a delightful young bloke in his early twenties with the oddly un-Russian name of Vladimir Schmidt. The son of a Russian nuclear physicist, he spoke English with a distinctly American accent as a consequence of learning the language from a groupie of Stalin's who'd arrived in Moscow from Minneapolis in the 1920s. Far from being KGB, he turned out to be a secret Christian who begged me to get him an English-language Bible.

When I asked Fred if I could have the office copy, he paled visibly and told me that it was clearly a case of entrapment. 'That's a favourite ploy of the KGB.' So Mr Schmidt had to wait until a subsequent visit for me to hand over the forbidden volume.

But this story concerns the night that Fred planned to throw us a party. Barry and I were to arrive at seven for seven-thirty and would meet the entire Australian population of the city, along with hand-picked members of the Soviet bureaucracy.

That day he could no longer lend us his car and chauffeur, but I'd found a rent-a-car company in Red Square. They had one car to rent. Its windscreen lacked wipers, its tyres tread and it was decades before the USSR would discover the seatbelt. The three of us set off in this woebegone vehicle and had an interesting day visiting onion-domed churches where frozen corpses, in open coffins, awaited the thaw so they could be buried with their antecedents.

With the Embassy's do only hours away, I volunteered to take Vladimir to his home – a high-rise on the outskirts of Moscow occupied entirely by nuclear physicists. (Just as nearby high-rises were occupied entirely by ballet dancers or approved-of novelists.) As we slipped and slithered through the dunes of snow, leaving Moscow further and further behind, I realised that we were at increasing risk. So it was a relief to say goodbye to Vlad and do a slithery U-turn and head back towards the faint lights of the great city. But about a mile down the road I managed to collide with the only other car we'd seen. It was a good solid thump and both our mudguards were stoved in.

That the only rent-a-car available in Moscow had had an accident with one of the only taxis provoked considerable interest. Within seconds, scores of people were struggling through the snowdrifts in the semi-darkness seeking amusement. Given that the temperature was forty below, it was quite clear that we were doomed to freeze to death and, after half an hour of being told to stay put, *'Nyet! Nyet! Militia!'* was the chorused advice, loudest of all from the taxi driver.

Barry was increasingly agitated because we were going to be late for Fred's fiesta. I was increasingly concerned because I knew that within the hour we'd be dead of hypothermia. With no sign of the militia, I decided to ignore the warnings and head for town. All but breaking off my frozen fingers, I managed to pull the crumpled mudguard from the bald tyre and started moving off while the crowd had conniptions.

Seconds later, the militia arrived. A black maria full of big blokes in grey uniforms with broad shoulders and heavily encrusted epaulets. Jones and Adams were arrested, tossed into the paddy wagon and taken to a police station where the cells were full of drunken Russians, US spies, counter-revolutionaries and, presumably, a few leftover capitalists.

We'd left our green diplomatic passports with Fred and, given the language difficulties, were finding it very hard to make friends with the fuzz. Their broad shoulders were not for crying on. They didn't like the look of us and it was clear we were heading for the gulag.

But it wasn't that that energised Barry so much as the thought of missing out on the Embassy party. Suddenly inspired, he discovered three or four words in Russian. *'Nyet touristi!'* he told them. *'Apparatchiks! Apparatchiks!'*

But the Russians were unpersuaded. Whereupon Barry got another inspiration and decided to convince them that we were not dangerous Americans but harmless Australians. So he started to leap around the place like a kangaroo. Far from convincing the authorities that we were from the Antipodes, it persuaded them that we were insane. Or at least that Barry was.

It took a few hours to sort things out and, finally, we were allowed to limp the Lada back to the Embassy. By then it was early in the morning, Fred and his staff were in a total panic and the disappearance of Barry and Phillip was on its way to making small headlines in the Australian newspapers.

To this day, whenever I see a kangaroo – and we've got thousands on the farm – I always think of Barry. *Nyet touristi! Kangaroo!*

On our return I wrote a one-page report to Gorton, which began with a nudge-nudge, wink-wink borrowing: 'We hold these truths to be self-evident. It is time to see our landscapes, hear our own voices and dream our own dreams.' The page set out a hypothetical three-step approach to creating a film industry. First, an experimental film fund to go fishing for young talent – prospective filmmakers would be given a few hundred dollars each to demonstrate their abilities. Second, the most promising youngsters would be sent to a national film school, where they would form creative teams and, on their graduation, would move on to stage three – a debut feature film funded by an Australian film development corporation.

Gorton ticked all the boxes – not even discussing it with his Cabinet – and the Australian film renaissance began. It would be Whitlam, however, who got to fully finance the proposal, after a determined effort by Bill McMahon's Arts Minister, Peter Howson (whom I always described as a 'pain in the arts'), to eliminate any initiative that could be identified with Gorton. But it was John who laid the foundation stone and who lived to see an Australian film industry surge onto our screens and those of the world. Gough always acknowledged John's role and invariably invited him to official occasions.

After decades of Hollywood dominance, we saw our own landscapes, heard our own voices and dreamt our own dreams.

When Jim Killen became Minister for the Navy, he made his first visit to HMAS *Melbourne* and detoured to the engine room in overalls. He spoke with a stoker and exchanged names.

'And what do you do?' the stoker asked.

'Well,' Jim replied, 'as a matter of fact I happen to be the Minister.'

Without batting an eyelid, the stoker looked at Jim and said, 'Smart bastard.'

Jim later wrote that this 'was one of the kindest things ever said to me and there were many times when I wished the summation was correct'.

At the end of his career Gorton returned to the backbench and was allocated a humble office in Parliament House. Old Parliament House. Barry Jones and I visited him to urge that he support Whitlam on a piece of legislation, even if it meant crossing the floor. After all, he owed nothing to the Liberal Party.

As he cogitated, my eyes passed over a number of photographs in silver frames that were placed, with heavy emphasis, on his desk. One was of Harold Wilson, with a fond personal inscription. The second, also personalised, was of the current Pope. And the third was of a distinguished-looking chap in a sort of Ruritanian military uniform, heavy with lanyards, epaulets with dangly things and an awesome variety of medals.

'Who's that?' I asked, pointing.

Gorton looked at the photograph for a long time. Though the photograph had clearly been a part of his décor for years, he seemed confused. Finally a confession. 'Buggered if I know!'

An hour later Barry, John and I stood on the steps of Old Parliament House – it was years before there'd be a new one – where, in a few months' time, Gough would talk about 'Kerr's cur'. The Aboriginal embassy was in the process of being established and Gorton gazed down bleakly. No better or worse than most MPs – on both sides of the House – he murmured, 'Inoperable cancer,' turned around and walked back into the building.

✆

With McMahon replacing Gorton in the Lodge, Jim Killen, a Gorton supporter, found himself given the order of the boot. In *Inside Australian Politics* Jim recalls being notified that the PM wanted to see him. 'I went to his office immediately,' he writes.

'"Good morning, Prime Minister," I said. He sat at his desk with his hands resting on the top. The moisture from his hands was clearly visible on the desk. He cleared his throat and began to speak, "I can't leave you . . . I can't leave you with the Navy."'

Killen protested. He loved the portfolio and asked, 'Why can't I stay?'

'You can't ask me that question,' McMahon replied irritably. 'I'm doing the decent thing and telling you personally rather than you read about it in the papers.'

'But I've been reading about it for the last week.'

Down the track, the diminutive PM made a strange confession while standing at the despatch box: 'I am my own worst enemy.'

From his exile on the backbench, the voice of Killen echoed through the chamber: 'Not while I'm alive!'

✆

In *A Certain Grandeur*, his epic book on the Whitlam years, Graham Freudenberg recalls Whitlam's response to Billy McMahon's efforts to oust John Gorton as Prime Minister. The campaign occurred at the same time as the BBC's *I, Claudius* was being screened in Australia. Emperor Tiberius was a central character.

Whitlam said of McMahon, 'He was determined, like other little Caesars, to destroy the Member for Higgins. There he sat, on the Isle of Capri at Surfers Paradise, plotting his destruction – Tiberius with a telephone.'

Graham Freudenberg agrees with McMahon's complaint that 'the press were far harder on him than Gorton'.

'For all his life-long cultivation of proprietors, McMahon's press support was minimal and grudging. His last prop was removed in 1972 when Sir Frank Packer sold the *Daily Telegraph* to Rupert Murdoch. Murdoch had committed his papers to a change of government. He telephoned McMahon in London to tell him of his deal with Packer: "I can promise, Prime Minister, that we'll be as fair to you as you deserve." In the background, Packer warned: "If you do that, you'll murder him."'

Barry Jones invited Ralph Nader to Australia shortly after the young Washington lawyer had written *Unsafe at Any Speed*, the book that wreaked havoc in Detroit as GM and Ford tried to deal with his relentless criticism of their products. Another Nader tour would follow and Ralph would leave behind him a more militant attitude amongst consumers.

Years later there'd be a sequel to those trips. When Gorbachev was trying to promote *glasnost* and *perestroika*, he realised that the Soviet customer was supine, too afraid to complain about anything. Constantly the range, the style, the durability and the reliability of Russian consumer goods was abysmal. What Gorby wanted was an alert, critical consumer to shake up Soviet manufacturing and retailing. So he invited Nader to Moscow and Nader invited Barry.

For me, the highlight of Nader's visits to Australia was one farewell dinner held at Melbourne University and attended by John Gorton, Graham Perkin (then editor of *The Age*), Gordon Barton (the IPEC entrepreneur who was in the process of forming his own political party) and the Australian Nobel laureate in physiology/medicine, Sir Macfarlane Burnet, and his wife, who was slowing dying of leukaemia. By this time Nader's interests extended far beyond Detroit, and 'Nader's Raiders' had attacked many aspects of American capitalism, including the banking system.

Mac was angry with Gorton for his advocacy of nuclear power – people forget that John was well on his way to establishing a nuclear power plant on the outskirts of Sydney when he lost power. Its foundations can still be seen in the grass at Jervis Bay. Nuclear power, Mac warned, would be a catastrophe for mankind. There was the problem of stations producing material to aid the proliferation of weapons. There was the risk of terrorism – Mac imagined hijackers seizing a Boeing and turning it into a suicide bomber by flying it into the core of a nuclear facility. He also talked about the intractable problem of waste and the medical dangers of radioactivity, his urgency seeming intensified by his wife's terminal illness. There would, Mac warned, be a vast increase in the incidence of cancers.

What, then, was the alternative? I asked Mac about wave power, currently much discussed. He reminded us that the moon exerted a gravitational pull on the earth which produced the tides – and insofar as you take power from the oceans you will pull the moon closer to our planet. Just a fraction at a time but, in due course, it would represent a problem. He was similarly unenthusiastic about wind power, saying there was no way to predict the negative effects of having thousands of giant windmills along a coast. By taking power from the wind, they would destroy the wind. What would happen on the other side of their giant blades?

No, the only answer was solar. And Mac drew a diagram on the university's white tablecloth. He described a collection of solar panels covering 100 square miles in the middle of the Nullarbor. 'Even with existing technology,' he said, 'such a solar collector could gather enough electricity for the entire planet.' Such an effort should become Australia's national obligation – an undertaking that could dwarf the Snowy Mountains Scheme in scale and symbolism.

Nader was entranced. He left the dinner, returned to America and added his opposition to nuclear power to Nader's Raiders' inventory of issues. There's an argument that Nader's energies opposing nuclear energy stopped the industry in its tracks, since no power plant was built after his return from Australia.

(Despite my friendship with James 'Gaia' Lovelock, who now argues that climate change has transformed the argument – that nuclear power may be the 'least worst' alternative for some nations – I'm still in Mac's court. Nuclear power is a cure that's worse than the disease.)

Slightly sozzled by this stage, John wasn't very eloquent in his own defence. Now, decades later, the nuclear power barrow is being pushed very energetically – both here and in the USA.

I have a framed letter on the wall of my office – from Bill McMahon at the Lodge. It's about an interview he had with David Frost, and he'd signed off with a cheerful flourish and 'Sonia sends her love'. This struck me as quite odd given that, at the time, I'd never met Sonia. But soon another rush of affection would be communicated to me by Liberal kingmaker Tony Staley.

Tony Staley, power behind the throne and puller of strings, rings me. 'I have a message from the Prime Minister.'

'What is it?'

'No, I have to deliver it in person. Can I take you to lunch?'

What could Bill McMahon possibly have to say to me?

Next day, a Commonwealth car (and I speak of a time when they were black) rolled up to my office and Tony swept me off to the Walnut Tree, in its day Melbourne's poshest restaurant, where he gave me quick instructions on which knife and fork to use. Then the messenger gave me the message. Or rather, issued the invitation.

'The Prime Minister would like you to become his media guru. He would like you to move to Canberra and live in the Lodge.'

I looked at Tony in disbelief.

'Work for McMahon?'

'Yes.'

'Live in the Lodge?'

'But I'm a Labor supporter.'

'He doesn't mind.'

'But I'm always insulting him.'

'He just laughs.'

'Last week I described him as looking like a Volkswagen with both doors open.'

'He thought that was funny.'

'And when he was in Washington with Sonia and Nugget Coombs in tow, I said, "Mrs McMahon looks like Snow White down to her last two dwarfs."'

Mrs McMahon thought that was funny.

'But I've got a business to run.'

'Take a leave of absence.'

'And I can't leave Melbourne and move to Canberra – what about my family?'

In effect, I was being offered a sort of membership in a surreal ménage. Nugget Coombs would be principal guru on matters political, and I would be guru two, guiding the Prime Minister's relationships with the print, radio and television media.

'Tony, this will cause a scandal. Bill will be eaten alive!'

Remaining calm, Tony made me promise I'd think about it. Sadly, I couldn't keep a secret and told the story to a nonplussed readership, which, I suspect, dismissed it as social satire.

The invitation was consequently withdrawn but, strangely, I remained on remarkably good terms with Bill. And with Sonia.

Years passed. It had been a long day and I needed a nap. So as I returned to my home away from home, the Sebel Townhouse in Sydney, where I told reception, 'No phone calls, please, unless it's the Prime Minister.' This was a joke.

Ten minutes later I was deeply asleep when the phone rang and an apologetic switchboard said, 'I know you said "unless it's the Prime Minister" – does that apply to an *ex*-Prime Minister?'

'Which one?'

'Sir William McMahon.'

It had been a long time since I'd heard from Bill. Curious, I said, 'Put him through.'

It was the voice of Bill's aide-de-camp, who, in a very proper baritone, sought confirmation that I was, in fact, Mr Adams and confirmed that Sir William wanted a word. There were a few clicks. Some more clicks. And then silence. Bill must have changed his mind. I hung up and went back to sleep.

A few minutes later the same sequence was repeated. The switchboard, the aide-de-camp, a promised connection to Sir William. Once again, clicks and silence.

So I hung up and jiggled the phone for the switchboard to say, 'No calls, no matter who they're from,' when Bill's go-between returned, apologised and said, yet again, 'Sir William.' Whereupon I heard a familiar, wavery voice saying, 'Hello? Hello?'

And I said, 'Hello, Bill.'

'Who's that?' said the squeaky voice.

'Phillip.'

'Phillip who?'

'Phillip Adams.'

'Why are you calling me, Phillip?'

'Bill, I'm not calling you. You're calling me.'

Another silence, suggesting that, yet again, we'd been disconnected. But then Bill said, 'Oh, yes, I remember. I want a favour.'

'I'll be happy to help if I can.'

And suddenly I was, once again, his media guru.

'I've written my autobiography and I want you to read it before I send it to the publishers. To tell me what you think.'

Bill's autobiography? I had no idea he'd been writing one. So I promised I would read it as soon as possible. I gave Bill my postal address, which he was clearly having problems writing down. And after much repeating of street names, numbers and postcodes, he said his aide-de-camp would courier it immediately.

On its arrival, I riffled through the pages somewhat uneasily. There was no doubt that Bill had an extraordinary story to tell – of his interactions with Gorton, Murdoch, and his mortal enemy, John McEwen, the leader of the Country Party. The endless machinations of the Liberal Party could be laid bare, and there'd be some amusing stories about him and Sonia and Richard Nixon.

But what I read was bad beyond belief. Appallingly written, not simply self-serving but entirely fictional, it was, in my view, unpublishable. When I spoke to Bill a few days later – by then he seemed to have forgotten both the book and my agreement to advise on it – he listened patiently to my gentle suggestion about a rewrite, a skilled editor, a ghost writer.

I later learned that he ignored my advice and proffered the book to a number of publishers, each of whom turned it down. I have, perhaps, the only copy in existence. Or rather, I had. I lent it to Barry Jones, who, uncharacteristically, lost it. It's somewhere in Barry's 'papers' but he's never been able to track it down. About the only literary effort that survives Bill is a book called *The Wit and Wisdom of William McMahon*, a small paperback with blank pages.

Barry Jones attended the funeral of our mutual friend John Gorton at St Andrew's Cathedral, Sydney, on 31 May 2002. It was, by any measure, an eclectic gathering, with the Whitlams, Frasers and Hawkes sitting together whilst Barry was in the company of some former Gorton Ministers. Tom Hughes QC, once Gorton's Attorney-General, delivered the eulogy, which, to everyone's astonishment, involved a savage attack on Malcolm Fraser that focused on his modus operandi in removing Gorton from the prime ministership. Barry was 'conscious of a rumble of approval around me' but felt sympathy for Malcolm.

After the service Bob Hawke's eyes were aglow. 'Those Liberals! They're such haters!' he told Barry. 'We're like Sunday school kids by comparison.'

Hawke, too, is a passionate hater. I know. He hates me. And he was implacably hostile to Barry Jones. Once when Jones was on the outer and I was hosting Hawke at an Australian film premiere, I spoke up on his behalf: 'You've got to remember, he's the most asked-for Labor personality at any party function – comes a close second to you – and he's widely considered to be the brainiest bloke in Parliament.'

It was the final suggestion that provoked Hawke's outburst. His denigration of Barry was very nasty. The subtext was clear. The smartest bloke in the Australian Parliament was the bloke yelling at me.

After a surly greeting from Gough (another 'Ah, Jim Cairns' campaign manager'), he, Clyde Holding and I climb into a black Commonwealth car and head for Geelong. In the proud tradition of Chifley, a railway employee is standing for Corio. He's a big boofy bloke called Gordon Scholes.

(Gordon would be Speaker at the time of the Dismissal – and when the House hastily passed several motions of confidence in the Whitlam Government he was instructed to relay their gist to the Governor-General. But at this time he was simply a candidate, fresh from working in the railways. Like the sainted Chifley, Scholes had been a choof-choof driver.)

Corio has been a difficult seat for Labor. Bob Hawke had stood in Corio – and was defeated – in 1963. Now, Gough is determined to make his mark there.

The drive to Geelong is tense and quiet. I was being sent to Coventry over Cairns. And when we arrive at a small, shabby fibro hall I'm fascinated by the people who crowd in. This is not the working class of socialist realism or Labor romanticism. These are not Hero Workers. The men and women who shuffle in look like Rowlandson engravings. Almost all are shabby and overweight.

Gough misreads their mood and needs and, as often happens, delivers a speech of mind-numbing dullness and technicalities. Indeed, it isn't a speech at all. It's the sort of lecture you might give to a room full of political students at the ANU. He's not only losing their attention but losing them physically. Quite a few clamber out of their seats and head for the doors.

To head off disaster, Clyde grabs the microphone from Gough and starts snarling into it. He seems to have shoved it up his nostril like a Ford Inhaler and the result is a high-pitched nasal whine. But it works. Those seeking escape turn back, resume their seats and Clyde gives them what they came to hear. A man-the-barricades, storm-the-Winter Palace harangue.

I can't forget the night because it was so characteristic of Whitlam. On one occasion he would raise his voice to the heavens and be Churchillian, Lincolnian, Shakespearean. Just as often he would drone on and on and on until his audience was comatose.

The scene is the old West Melbourne Stadium, usually filled by crowds cheering such legendary wrestlers as Chief Little Wolf or booing disastrous Judy Garland concerts. On this occasion, a star of far greater magnitude dominates the stage beneath an 'It's Time' banner. He is, of course, Gough Whitlam, in his best 'Men and women of Australia' mode. 'Time for this, time for that,' chorus the celebrities, and Gough stands before us, our Messiah.

I'm standing up the back with Frank Crean, who would, in due course, become Gough's Deputy Prime Minister. The rising frenzy of the crowd has made us both reflective. An underwhelmed Frank shakes his head and, almost sadly, says, 'It's worse than the Nuremberg Rally.'

Australian elections were now utterly, entirely and expensively presidential. The die has been cast.

John Button told me of Whitlam's supercilious conduct at his first fully fledged Cabinet meeting in 1972. 'He looked around at us, studying our faces one by one. And then he said, "None of you cunts matter."'

Decades later I asked Gough if he would authenticate the story. 'Comrade, I would never, never use that word.' Then he reconsidered. 'Except, perhaps, on one occasion. A Member of the Opposition, afflicted by a stammer, was attempting to say, "I am a Country Party member." But he couldn't get past "I'm a cunt, cunt, cunt . . ." And I tried to help him out by saying, "But we all knew that."'

Barry Jones' autobiography, *A Thinking Reed*, is a rich source of Labor history and of observations on the Great Leader. 'The Hansard Index records Gough Whitlam's outstanding industry,' wrote Barry. 'He spoke more and asked or answered more questions on a far wider range of subjects than any Member in the history of the House of Representatives. Working on an average of 72 items in each column of the Index, I calculated that in the ten years 1969 to 78 Whitlam made 11,360 contributions. The highest number was in 1971 (2412 entries) and the lowest in 1978 (580), the year he resigned.'

Barry observed that the numbers fell in the years of his prime ministership because he was limited to answering questions and unable to ask them, 'which must have been frustrating'.

In *Gough Whitlam: A Moment in History*, Jenny Hocking relates what happened in September 1965, when Whitlam erupted in a parliamentary debate. The topic? Extending repatriation benefits to Salvation Army members who'd served in combat arenas.

As Jenny writes, 'The Minister for External Affairs, Paul Hasluck, whose parents had been Salvation Army officers, had not even spoken during the debate . . . Whitlam was tired and churlish when he cruelly accused Hasluck of denying justice to his own parents . . . the two men were seated opposite each other, barely a metre apart. As Whitlam, still standing, began to drink from a glass of water on the table in front of him, Hasluck leaned forward and retorted, "You're one of the filthiest speakers I've ever heard in this Chamber". In that moment, Whitlam tossed the contents of his glass over Hasluck. A great hush fell as the water, and the colour, drained from Hasluck's face. He took a hankie from his top pocket and mopped it.'

Jenny records the subsequent insults: 'Wetty Whitlam' and 'Waterboy'.

As the world tilted on its axis and Whitlam took the reins, I took Barry Humphries to Parliament House. It was his first time. The visit remains memorable for two reasons. Humphries got us both into trouble – almost evicted from the premises – when we were invited into the ABC's tiny booth. Here announcers provided murmured voiceovers – identifying whoever is speaking as the Member for Higgins or whatever. In the midst of a murmur, Barry grabbed the microphone and started proffering irreverent embellishments.

Outside in King's Hall, when the fuss had died down, I introduced Humphries to a number of political notables. With an ear to accent as acute as Professor Higgins, and a comparable ability to identify social pretensions, Humphries was fascinated by the mixed signals from MPs. Thus Andrew Peacock, with his Toorak address and Portsea tan, said, 'G'day, mate,' as he shook the Humphries hand. And a Labor MP, Gordon Scholes, promoted to politics from the railways, tried to sound like a graduate of Melbourne Grammar. Clearly the Alf Garnett phenomenon I'd observed in the Labor Party when Arthur Calwell was still the leader had won the day – with many in the party of the proletariat yearning for posh.

Not long after Barry Humphries gatecrashed the ABC's booth in federal Parliament, Spike Milligan and the Goons followed suit. But their attacks on the dignity of proceedings were entirely inadvertent.

I happened to be listening to a particularly dull debate when, to my astonishment, I heard the famous Eccles and Bluebottle join proceedings. For a couple of minutes the cast of *The Goon Show* wandered in and out of the House of Reps, their voices so perfectly blending with the MPs' that one expected terms like 'the dreaded deadings' to be included in *Hansard*. Clearly someone was deliberately fading the Goons in and out, and doing it very skilfully.

Investigations revealed there had been a problem in the mysterious complex known as 'master control', where all ABC programs are bounced around the country – and where interviews are pre-recorded. Never before, or since, has Parliament sounded better.

Except, perhaps, for another fragment of a parliamentary broadcast I heard a few months later. In the dying days of the Whitlam Government there was a debate on mining – perhaps the mining of uranium, though I can't be sure – and I hadn't been paying much attention. But suddenly there was a new contributor to the debate and, within seconds, I was on the edge of my seat.

The voice coming out my transistor was full of cheek and chutzpah, witheringly contemptuous of the Libs. There was a whiff of gunpowder, something exciting and dangerous about this bloke. I'd never heard the voice before and had no idea who he was.

Then the anonymous voice in the ABC booth identified him. 'The Minister for Northern Australia, Paul Keating.' The Dismissal was only days away but, of course, I didn't know that. Nor could I guess that Keating would, pretty soon, prove himself to be the most fascinating politician of his generation.

From day one, Paul Keating was disinclined to tug the forelock. Not even to the awe-inspiring Whitlam. Having failed to make the cut for Gough's 1972 ministry, he maintained at best brittle relations. Whitlam once approached Keating and said, 'That was a good speech. You should go back, comrade, and get yourself an honours degree.'

Keating snarled, 'What for? Then I'd be like you.'

And when the Great Man was trying to recruit MPs for a Caucus vote, Keating said, icily, 'You need me more than I'll ever need you.'

⁓

Barry Cohen's political career culminated with a ministry (Arts, Heritage and the Environment) in the two Hawke Governments. Equally important was his thirty-year stint as an unofficial amanuensis for Gough Whitlam, collecting and collating stories of the leader for a series of popular paperbacks. Cohen and I had been friends for much of the same period – but that all ended with 9/11.

When I wrote a column urging Australia to proceed with caution – not to be swept up in what I feared would be the irrationalities of the Bush response – Barry cast me into the outer darkness. Regarding any criticism of the USA as, in effect, hostile to Israel, he has never spoken to me again.

Previously, I'd helped Barry with his books – contributing stories, writing introductions and cutting the ribbons at his launches. Thus, versions of some of the Whitlam stories that follow appear in one or more of Barry's books. Others come from the same sources – conversations, memories and newspaper clippings.

⁓

Carol Summerhayes was Gough's private secretary during his period as Leader of the Opposition and then Prime Minister. When he criticised her attempts to turn his utterances into text, she said, 'I can't read your bloody mind.'

'Well, speak to someone who can.'

❧

On becoming PM, Whitlam put the old prime ministerial Bentley out to pasture. He would, in future, be driven in a democratic Ford or Holden from the car pool.

Yet in 1973 he surprised the troops by ordering a huge white Mercedes, a model unique in Australia. It cost a fortune. When responding to criticisms during question time, Gough defended himself by saying he'd be 'happy if every office-bearer in Parliament were to make do with an ordinary Holden or Valiant, but if there's to be any gradation of cars then, quite frankly, I'm going to have the best.'

It might have been more tactful had Gough defended himself by emphasising that he was six-foot-four.

❧

In an effort to look prudent with taxpayers' funds, the Whitlam Government told its MPs and Senators that they'd have to fly economy instead of first-class.

In response to complaints at a Cabinet meeting, Whitlam said, 'Most of the people around this table are pissants, and they can travel first-class for the rest of their lives and they'll still be pissants. I, on the other hand, could travel economy-class forever and still be a great man!'

❧

Whitlam often talked about his ability to walk on water, provoking Bill Hayden to observe that, had the Prime Minister strolled across Lake Burley Griffin in 1975, a hostile media would have published the story under the headline 'Gough Can't Swim'.

On Gough's first trip to Europe as Prime Minister, he decided to grant the Pope an audience. Staff-member Eric Welsh took sets of rosary beads to be blessed by His Holiness – for himself and Federal Secretary Mick Young. Whitlam wondered why he bothered. 'You needn't have gone to all that trouble, Eric – I could have blessed them myself.'

Question time.

A Dorothy Dixer: 'It has been said you are the best thing the Labor Government has going for it. What would happen to the Government if you fell under a bus tomorrow?'

Whitlam: 'With the improvements my Government has initiated in urban transport, this is unlikely to happen.'

Graham Freudenberg, speechwriter to many a Labor great and a man who seemed to become Gough through a process of osmosis, recalls the odd disagreement. As when Gough complained of Graham's writing style with the observation that 'you, comrade, are too dithyrambic, while I am too inspissated'.

On checking, Freudenberg found that 'dithyrambic' pertains to a vehement hymn, whilst 'inspissated' means dense and thick.

In his later years Clyde Cameron became a regular correspondent of mine, and somewhere I've a collection of his letters. Just as US mythology says you can go from a log cabin to the White House, Clyde went from a shearing shed to Gough Whitlam's front bench, becoming the Minister for Labour, Immigration and Consumer Affairs in the Whitlam Government.

Described by Hawkey as a 'great hater', Clyde's tendency to thumb his nose provoked Whitlam to sack him from the front bench in 1975. During a discussion on economics, Clyde's disagreements angered the PM. 'What would a fucking ex-shearer know about economics?'

'As much as a classical Greek scholar,' said Clyde.

Jim Killen on Whitlam: 'I reached the firm conclusion that he would be the most perfect product of pomposity ever to emerge out of the upper-middle-class society and fasten himself leech-like onto the egalitarian movement.'

In *The Wit of Whitlam*, Deane Wells recalls that, during the 1974 double-dissolution election campaign, Whitlam 'never missed an opportunity to have a shot at the Leader of the Opposition, Billy Snedden'.

On one occasion he said, 'I want to assure the honourable gentleman that the bodyguards they can see accompanying the Leader of the Opposition are not to prevent other people shooting him but to prevent him shooting himself.'

❧

History, and Barry Cohen, record that Gough looked down on small men in more ways than one. Of the genre, only John Button seemed to measure up in Gough's regard. Cohen writes of 'one of the lesser giants, Dr Richie Gun' – the Member for Kingston, South Australia.

'Appearing with him at a rally in his electorate during the 1975 election campaign, Gough was idly thumbing through Richie's election pamphlet and noticed the following reference to both of them. "The Prime Minister has often stated his admiration for Dr Gun's wide general knowledge."

'Gough did a double-take and whispered to the local MP, "Gun, what's all this about? I've said no such thing."

'"Yes you did, Prime Minister," replied Richie, "you often call me a 'fucking little know-all'."'

❧

Senator Douglas 'Rubber Dougie' McClelland liked to tell the story of Gough's visit to a north-coast town in New South Wales. When the branch president tried to introduce the great man and his cohorts at a meeting, he became somewhat stumble-tongued. 'Ladies and gentlemen, distinctive guests, it's my pleasure to introduce the President of Australia, Mr Jeff Whitlam, and Senator Jim McClelland.'

Gough turned to Doug and whispered, 'Comrade, we're amongst savages.'

❧

I think my favourite Whitlam anecdote involves his attendance at a rugby match in Queensland. It was in 1974 and Gough's star was on the wane. His host was Ron McAuliffe, who doubled as a Labor Senator and the President of the Queensland Rugby League. As they walked together towards the centre of the ground, a huge crowd booed and hissed and jeered and catcalled – as well as tossing a variety of missiles.

On their way back to the stand, Gough turned to the very embarrassed Senator and said, 'McAuliffe, never again invite me to a place where you are so unpopular!'

❧

In *Trial Balance*, Nugget Coombs remembers Whitlam's 'exhibitions of temper at the expense of members of his staff'. He viewed them as 'calculated pieces of histrionics, part of Whitlam's tendency to act out, in a style exaggerated to the point of mockery, a kind of caricature of himself'.

Nonetheless, Nugget found them distressing to witness and remembers one senior staffer complaining, 'I notice you don't abuse Nugget the way you do the rest of us.'

Whitlam paused before replying. 'No, he's the sort of bastard who would walk out if I did.'

❧

Nugget Coombs was perhaps Australia's most distinguished public servant. He'd served every Prime Minister from Curtin to Whitlam and, as Chairman of the Reserve Bank, had signed all the money. Now, in 1972, he was to become Chairman of the Australia Council, Whitlam's transformed version of the Australian Council for the Arts. I was to be a board member and the chairman of one of the seven constituent boards, the Film and Television Board.

The Shadow Minister for the Arts had been Senator Douglas McClelland, aka Rubber Dougie, whom Nugget and I feared would be a disaster in the ministry. He was, after all, one of the models for Barry Humphries' Sir Les Paterson. So Nugget and I conspired in the writing of a letter to Whitlam (in which I addressed Gough as 'My dear Medici Prince'), urging him to split the portfolio. Let McClelland have Media, if he must, but please, Medici Prince, take the Arts on yourself.

There was more to the letter than escaping McClelland. André Malraux, when acting as Minister of Culture for President Charles de Gaulle, told Nugget to 'get the President to keep the Arts to himself. Then you will get the money and he will be too busy to interfere. Whereas a junior Minister? He will not get the money and will always interfere.'

Correspondence between Gough and myself was frequently facetious. I'd write to Prince Hal and he would reply to Falstaff. But the Medici reference was clearly effective. When Gough announced his ministry he confirmed McClelland as Minister for the Media but – praise be! – took the role of being Australia's cultural benefactor. He would run the renaissance.

Malraux was right. And so were Nugget and I. Whitlam would heap the sort of money on the arts that, more recently, Rudd would heap upon an ailing economy. As far as the arts were concerned,

Whitlam's munificence proved to be the most successful stimulus package in history.

∿

For a while things worked very well. I had a blank cheque for resurrecting Australian film but, increasingly, had rows with Nugget's CEO, Dr Jean Battersby. She thought I was uncontrollable and I thought her stultifying view bureaucratic. So I went to see Nugget, determined to resign.

Cecily, Nugget's lifelong secretary, began each day by shuffling through Nugget's favourite quotations, which she'd typed onto cards, and selecting one to slip into a small frame on his desk. On this occasion, I think he'd made his own choice. Before I could launch into my tirade against Jean (who later became one of my dearest friends), he rotated the frame and nodded to the maxim: 'Never, never, NEVER resign. Once you resign you're fucked. Ben Chifley.'

So I didn't.

As the years passed, I saw more and more of Nugget, joining with him and Judith Wright to campaign for a treaty with the Aboriginal people. I'd interview Nugget on the wireless or, as he became feebler in his old age, take him for drives. My last memory of him remains one of the most intense of my life.

He was imprisoned in a multi-storey gulag on the North Shore of Sydney, the sort of place Dame Edna once described as a 'high-security nursing home'. The overworked nurses, with no glimmering of the status of their guest, treated him like a five-year-old. How had it come to this? Surely we could do better for our tribal elders?

By now Nugget could only repeat things you said to him. Which he did with intensity, as though he were initiating the conversation rather than echoing it. Finally, it was time to leave and Nugget suddenly reached up, grabbed me by the shoulder and pulled me down. So that he could kiss me. On the lips. I was both astonished and humbled.

There was desperation as well as affection in that embrace. He was taking the advice of Chifley. Never, never resign. Least of all from life itself.

Though happy to be a warrior for the nascent film industry, Whitlam was destined to lose his nerve when his towering personage was challenged by a Toulouse-Lautrec of US politics.

Jack Valenti had been a hatchet man for Lyndon Johnson, Hubert Humphrey and the Kennedys – something between a bagman and a spear carrier. His reward was a sinecure running the Motion Picture Association of America – one of that nation's most powerful lobby groups. God help any country that challenged the US film industry. He would transform the 'soft power' of US influence into the hard power of punishment. If the French or the Indians – let alone the Australians – took Hollywood on, he'd threaten massive retaliation. This usually involved not-very-veiled threats of trade embargoes in entirely different areas – such as cutting off the importation of our beef and lamb.

And Valenti was an old friend of Doug McClelland.

Getting an Australian film industry up and running required, at the same time, a bolstering of the TV production sector. And the networks just weren't interested. Their defence? They couldn't afford to produce Australian program material. They had no money left after they'd bought all the *F.B.I.*s and *Mister Ed*s.

If there was any truth in this, it was entirely the networks' own fault. Each week they'd send senior people to Los Angeles to bid against each other at what was, effectively, an auction sale of US TV product. As a result of the bidding, the prices soared until Australia was paying far more per capita than any other nation. In absolute terms, we were as big a market for Hollywood as the UK or Germany.

Having persuaded the Government to have a Tariff Board inquiry into an industry which effectively didn't exist, I decided to unveil my cunning plan on the very last day of the hearings. Nugget and I fronted together, with me revealing to Richard Boyer an idea of elegant simplicity. Instead of allowing the Hollywood studios to laugh all the way to their respective banks, Australia would stop the networks attending the auction. Instead, we'd send an official buying agent to the States armed with the shopping list of programs nominated by the networks. With no other bidders, the agent would buy the US products at knockdown prices and return triumphantly to our shores. A local auction would then be held, where the local networks could bid as stupidly as they wished. But the profits wouldn't go to Hollywood. They'd go into a production fund for local television.

As the last cabs off the rank, Nugget and I made a powerful impression on Richard, who made the buying agency the central idea in his report. It was kept under wraps until it could be discussed by Cabinet, but someone leaked it to the Dream Factory's diminutive dictator. I've long suspected that the leak came from a Whitlam Minister who was no friend of mine.

Valenti was outraged. He discovered that Whitlam was returning to Canberra after one of his circumnavigations of the planet and flew to Honolulu to confront him in a passenger lounge. Valenti told Whitlam that if the Adams plan was approved, Australia would never see another American television program again and, as well, we'd be denied access to Hollywood feature films.

Whitlam immediately grew uncharacteristically wobbly and reported his encounter to the Cabinet. They immediately surrendered.

Valenti's threat was fatuous. It wouldn't have lasted ten minutes. Not only was Australia an indispensable market to the USA but we're talking of a time when independent filmmakers were breaking down the totalitarian era of the big studios. A brief embargo would have served to anger Australians by making America's cultural imperialism self-evident, which would have generated even more support for Australian film and television producers.

But Valenti had cut Whitlam down to size – one of the few people who ever managed to do so.

Valenti died a few years back. A few days before they rolled his end credits, I got a letter from him complaining about a column I'd written on US cultural hegemony. We'd been sparring partners for forty years, ever since meeting in his New York office (his other was, of course, in Washington). The office wall was covered in autographed photographs of the giants of the Democratic Party and its White House incumbents. They were getting a little old and tatty but it was still a formidable array. Valenti with Johnson. Valenti with Humphrey. Valenti with the Kennedy brothers. And, of course, Valenti with every Hollywood star since, it would seem, Valentino.

At one point during our terse meeting he left the office to take a phone call from Washington. In his absence, I couldn't resist the temptation to lean forward and open the thick folder on his desk. It was a dossier on me. Far, far thicker than ASIO's. It could only have been compiled by the FBI. No, not the series starring Efrem Zimbalist, Jr, but the original production starring J. Edgar Hoover.

To dramatise the notion of US 'soft power', I would later write that 'Paramount is as powerful as the Pentagon, Metro as mighty as the White House'. Hyperbole? Understatement. The cultural dominance of Hollywood for much of the twentieth century was as crucial to US power as its military. Australia was not alone in dragging the Trojan Horse of Hollywood into our cinemas but, thanks to television, we had also dragged it into our very lounge rooms.

With Whitlam backing the strategy Barry Jones and I had outlined to Gorton, the building blocks for an Australian film industry are put in place. The Experimental Film Fund would be followed by the Australian Film Development Corporation and a National Film and Television School.

Don Dunstan is the first state Premier to sense an opportunity. He invites me to Adelaide and I'm ushered into his large corner office. It's our first meeting. Backlit, he walks towards me and extends a hand on which there's a ring heavily burdened with a lump of turquoise. I'm not sure whether I should shake the hand or kiss the ring.

He then ushers me to a conversation pit beneath the obligatory Fred Williams. But before beginning our discussion he turns on a large Grundig radio. As the volume of sound makes conversation difficult, I suggest he turn it down. Better still, off. Don shakes his head, pointing to the wall. 'The permanent head is eavesdropping.' Apparently he's on the other side, his ear pressed to a glass tumbler, which, in turn, is pressed to the wall. Clearly, Dunstan is finding it difficult to deal with bureaucrats still loyal to Sir Thomas Playford.

Don explains that he wants to become a part of the new film industry. First of all, he asks me to come and live in Adelaide. I explain this is impossible. Then he tells me he's in negotiation with the Fuji film company, which is willing to open a processing laboratory in Adelaide. 'We could do all the rushes for the films in Melbourne and Sydney.' I explain that 'rushes' mean what they say – that there's a necessity of a quick turnaround. With long flights in either direction it's not going to work.

Instead, we decide that South Australia should get into film production itself. But by stealth. A South Australian Film Corporation will bring together the little pockets of film production in various ministries, a manoeuvre that will camouflage our real intent – to make features! We'll invite the best and brightest over from Melbourne and Sydney and have them educate the few local filmmakers 'on the job'. Thus, the SAFC is born and, before anyone has woken up to the strategy, it is making *Sunday Too Far Away* and *Picnic at Hanging Rock*.

Don's example is followed by the Premiers of Victoria, Tasmania, Queensland and New South Wales. Only the Western Australians are slow to respond. Having made local production close to impossible, Australia now makes it all too easy. Suddenly welcome mats are out everywhere.

My friendship with Dunstan was off to a flying start – although it would have its strains and tensions. During a time of increasing speculation about his sexuality, he phones with the news that he's impregnated a woman who was something of a legend in artistic circles. (She'd recently told friends that 'I'm going to fuck my way to the Lodge'.) 'What should I do?' asks Don. Knowing it would put an end to the rumours, I suggest that he call a press conference.

The crisis ends with a miscarriage and, down the track, Don marries for the second time. To some of us, the nuptials with Adele Koh seem intended to deflect attention from the whispers. But after her death from cancer, another reason for the wedding emerges.

One of Don's closest friends tells me how the grief-stricken bloke was quietly reading Adele's diaries when he came upon entries that further shattered him. Don's intimates knew that he'd married Adele in the belief that she was pregnant. Whereas her diary made it clear that that her condition was fictitious. Even worse, Don learned that she had continued having an affair with a colleague.

The innuendo and accusations about Dunstan's homosexuality escalate until, finally, he stops arguing. And the final years of his life, well and truly out of the closet, are more serene.

Arthur Augustus Calwell was born in 1896 and died in 1973, within the first year of the Whitlam Government. He'd had a very long, turbulent and often significant career and was one of the few Australian politicians to survive an assassination attempt. In 1966 a deranged nineteen-year-old, Peter Kocan, had shot him in the face with a sawn-off shotgun. Arthur had set an example that Jim Cairns would follow later – by forgiving his assailant.

He was buried in Melbourne's General Cemetery alongside his son, Arthur Andrew, who had died of leukaemia at the age of eleven. Those close to Arthur say that he never recovered from the tragedy. His funeral in Melbourne was to be a great tribal occasion, and although I wasn't attending I found myself on a flight south from Canberra which was crowded with mourners.

One of them, a very small and very old man, sat beside me. He introduced himself as Jack Dedman. Like Arthur, he'd been born in 1896 and would die within weeks of his old comrade. I thought he'd been dead for decades.

Jack had become a member of the ALP in the late 1920s, read economics in the early 1930s and would emerge as one of the party's most radical voices on banking. He'd contested federal and state seats in the 1930s and, with the approach of war, had enrolled as a part-time student at the University of Melbourne so as to better understand the economic theories of Keynes.

His physical frailty seemed to fade as we flew to Melbourne. He was energised by Arthur's death and needed to talk. I was happy to be his audience as he remembered the years when John Curtin had elevated him to his wartime Cabinet. Amongst his portfolios he was Minister for War Organisation of Industry, and he became a full member of the War Cabinet. In 1945 he succeeded Chifley as Minister for Postwar Reconstruction and was responsible for the Snowy Mountains Scheme, the Universities Commission and the Australian National University.

I was riveted by the stories Jack told and begged him not to waste them on an audience of one. 'You must write your autobiography!'

'I am,' he said. 'I'm working on it. I spend a lot of time in the parliamentary library.'

Around five months later I was distressed by the news of

Dedman's death. The book would never be written, though others would celebrate his life – and the National Library has a long interview with him recorded in the 1960s.

But none of the academic writings on the old bloke – nor the National Library transcript – are as evocative as what I heard on that brief flight. This reminds me of the poverty of Australian political literature. Nugget Coombs would have a crack at biography but he was so inhibited by a lifetime of tactfulness that the results verged on the infuriating. As I complained to him at the time, 'You're too nice to too many people.'

Australia needs more political diaries. We have so few, and even the most infuriating of them – Peter Howson's comes to mind – are nonetheless invaluable.

A great deal of history died with Calwell. More died with Dedman. And unless Paul Keating gets off his backside and writes his autobiography, much more will die with him.

For a couple of years I was, in effect, the Melbourne *Herald*'s political cartoonist. But the Melbourne *Herald* knew nothing about it. They thought the cartoons they were publishing were the work of Peter Russell-Clarke. Little did they know that Peter would disturb my slumbers with desperate cries for help. 'Christ, what am I going to do today? You've got to help me!'

Let it be said that cartoonists are, by and large, the most eccentric members of what used to be the Fourth Estate. These days, 'estate' takes on an increasingly funereal, post-mortem meaning, but we're talking of a time when people still read newspapers, when they dominated public debate. Even the most conservative masthead would employ and tolerate cartoonists of recalcitrant, even reprehensible behaviour. And of them all, Peter was the wildest. Has Leak ever leaked into his editor's in-tray? Peter did.

Peter was already notorious as a latter-day bohemian and satyr and would, down the track, become a famous chef, an antecedent to Gordon Ramsay. But when it came to political cartooning he had a problem. He knew nothing about politics. Hence the desperate phone calls by the dawn's early light. In a couple of hours he'd have to present alternative sketches to the editor in the hope that one would get an approving grunt, even a chuckle. Bleary-eyed and bleary-eared, I'd try to help.

I'd ask Peter to tell me what stories the paper was preparing and would patiently explain who Trudeau was or why Clyde Cameron detested Gough. And, like a spirit guide with a ouija board, I'd guide Peter's pencil over his pad and suggest words to go with the drawings. This farce continued until I was too sleep-deprived to continue – so I found Peter a new career on television. Promoting eggs for the Victorian Egg Board and preparing improbable dishes on *The Don Lane Show*.

Because we both needed some R&R, I took Peter on one of my trips to Egypt. One of the highlights occurred in Luxor when, having exhausted the tombs of the kings, queens and nobles, I asked the most notorious tour guide for something off the beaten track.

Looking more like a Harlem pimp than an antiquities expert, he gazed at me through his reflective sunglasses and said he'd make arrangements for us to visit 'Cleopatra's tomb'. I knew this was nonsensical but was intrigued by his description of a major monument to Hathor a few hours' drive into the desert. And the eyes hidden behind the mirror lenses made a somewhat erroneous observation. He assumed that two bearded gentlemen travelling together had to be gay. So he tapped the side of his nose with his forefinger and said, 'And when you get there, you will get what you like.'

We had no idea what he meant. Perhaps genuine artefacts for a few Egyptian pounds? What he'd planned for us came as a terrible shock, which I described in a newspaper column. Peter and I arrived at Hathor's temple where, yes, there was a vestigial portrait of Cleopatra on an external wall. We were taken into its bat-filled bowels by a young bloke carrying a candle.

Just when the darkness could get no deeper, the prevailing stench of bats no more repulsive, he blew the candle out. And he threw his arms around and started kissing me with feigned passion. A struggle in the darkness ensued, but the more I protested and hit at him the more ardent became his attentions. I guess he was only trying to please. Having escaped his embraces, I stumbled through the darkness, falling up and down stairs, until I was once again in the blinding light of the desert.

A few months later a postcard bearing a Luxor postmark arrived from Egypt. Pure kitsch – pyramids, camels, Darrell Lea colours. And on the other side these words: 'Dear Phillip, your guide awaits your second coming. Knowing we were no match for you in the back passage, Margaret and I took a torch. Yours ever, Gough.'

In the early 1980s I climb on a flight from Cairo to Sydney and find John Button sitting beside me. John is still fuming with irritation at what he regards as the incompetence of our Cairo Embassy.

They hadn't organised the sort of meetings he wanted – he'd had to do it himself. And he makes a powerful point that, these days, embassies seem less and less relevant. There was a time when messages could take months to reach them, when an ambassador required and had considerable latitude and so had to be trusted to look after his nation's interests. But these days, communications were instantaneous and a Minister like Button could do a Henry Kissinger and conduct his business by jet.

Menzies liked to go to the UK on an ocean liner. Not only was it comfortable but, he insisted, he arrived at his destination rested and ready for anything. Whereas Kissinger? Five cities, five national capitals in five days? Crucial negotiations befuddled by jetlag?

When we arrive in Melbourne, John asks me if I mind smuggling some of his duty-free grog through customs.

Tullamarine. I'm rushing to catch a plane to Sydney and see John Button heading for the Comcar desk. He comes over, grabs my arm and says, in a quiet voice, 'My son is a junkie.' There's a silence and then he warns me to be very careful of my kids.

John and I live quite close to each other, in different parts of Hawthorn, one of Melbourne's leafier, safer, calmer suburbs. What he says seems impossible. A few months later Barry Jones phones. 'Get around to the Buttons' as soon as you can. His son is dead.'

David has taken an overdose in the back garden. When I arrive, the body has been removed and the Buttons and their surviving son, James, are sitting in silence. With nothing to say, I add to the silence.

John has talked to me about the great gap between him and the boy – their inability to communicate. Now he blames himself and his life as a politician for what has happened. He's convinced the dead boy despised him. James disagrees. 'You're wrong, Dad. I used to hear him in his bedroom at night reading your speeches from *Hansard*. Reading them out loud.'

Somehow this revelation adds to John's despair. He takes me into the dead boy's room. 'This is how a junkie lives.' It doesn't look much different to the bedrooms of any of my three daughters. The same spectacular mess. John picks up a book from the floor. It's a novel, popular at the time, called *The Dice Man*. John says, 'He lived by this wretched book.' As if to say he died by it.

The Dice Man? The central proposition is that choices are so arbitrary, and outcomes so unpredictable, that you might as well use a roll of the dice to make the big decisions, and the little ones.

My partner, Patrice Newell, forms the Climate Change Coalition, a small political party that will focus entirely on an issue that the major parties are trying to avoid. The Greens aren't very happy, but Patrice argues that they carry so much baggage on other issues that another fully focused group, with no stated views on drugs or foreign policy, might lift the aggregate vote.

She rounds up candidates all over Australia to contest the 2007 federal election. Karl Kruszelnicki becomes the best-known candidate and, despite being novices, they do pretty well. One of the first people to join the new party is John Button. In defiance of ALP rules, which regard such an act as a hanging offence. Button is quite public about it, and utterly unapologetic. He agrees that climate change is the most important issue of all. Let the ALP expel him if it wants to.

With Billy Snedden as Opposition Leader, the Liberals managed to lose an election against the wounded Whitlam. Billy Snedden proved to be as vulnerable to satire as 'Silly Billy' McMahon. I've still got a campaign badge put out by Labor with a Petty profile of Snedden topped by the admonition to 'Vote One: BOOFHEAD'. (Boofhead was a comic-strip character of the era – the apotheosis of stupidity.)

One of the most boofhead things Bill ever said would haunt him afterwards. When addressing a business lunch in Melbourne, he copped a narky question about the leadership and replied, 'I'll tell you why I should be leader of the Liberal Party – I'm the best. That's why I should be. I can give leadership to my team and they will all follow me. If I ask them to walk through the Valley of Death on hot coals they'd do it. Every one of them trusts me. Everyone recognises my political judgement, and if I say something must be this, it will be. That's why I'm leader.'

As Paul Kelly recalls, those words were hanging in the air when six Liberals went in a deputation to ask Snedden to resign. 'A party leader can only insult the intelligence and sensitivity of his colleagues so much.'

But in a strange way Snedden had the last laugh. Like another political failure, Nelson Rockefeller, Billy died during sexual intercourse with a mystery woman. The list of nominees for this femme fatale was long, celebrity-laden and slanderous. But it gave Bill the posthumous respect he could never achieve in life. 'On the job,' said one parliamentary colleague, 'and on the vinegar stroke! That's the only way to die.'

When launching a TV series by David Frost in Canberra, Gough was having trouble adjusting the microphone, which seemed afflicted by detumescence. 'I am always told,' he confided to the audience, 'that the harder you try the more it droops.'

I recently discovered a group photograph taken in 1972 on the lawns of Kirribilli House. The great occasion was the first meeting of the Australia Council. Gough, as a Medici prince, is surrounded by the likes of Nugget Coombs, Jean Battersby, David Williamson, Clifton Pugh and myself – all members of the wedding.

Of my distinguished colleagues on the Council, far and away the most infuriating – and strangely boring – was Pugh. A fine painter of dead kangaroos and living Prime Ministers, Pugh was more pompous than Gough on a bad day. He was, at the time, seeking to paint portraits of the most important people on earth – everyone from Zhou Enlai to the Duke of Edinburgh.

Infuriated by his nonsensical performances at Council meetings, I invented a character called Clayton Puff and wrote regularly about his efforts to achieve high-end subjects for his portraits. Clayton – sorry, Clifton – was not amused and nor was his energetic missus, Judith, whose seductive entreaties had landed many a big fish. (For example, in her recently published autobiography, Judith more than hints at an affair than Don Dunstan.)

A year later, Pugh's portrait of Gough won the Archibald and the PM sent him the following telegram: 'Your place in the history of politics, like mine in the history of art, has been assured.'

When Nugget retired, Clifton was determined to take over as Chairman of the Council. But Gough was disinclined to make an appointment that would have been as silly as Sir John Kerr's as GG. 'You may be the Michelangelo of our time,' the PM told Pugh, 'but don't forget that, for the present, I am Julius II.'

Later Pugh would claim that, whilst painting Sir John Kerr, he'd suddenly realised that the GG intended to assassinate the PM and had done his best to alert Whitlam to the danger. Thus he became like the voice in the crowd in Shakespeare's account of the assassination of Julius Caesar – warning of 'the Ides of November'. To be involved with Whitlam is to drown in classical references.

As Arts Minister, Barry Cohen made two auspicious appointments. I was anointed Chairman of the Australian Film Commission whilst Gough became Chairman of the National Gallery. Soon thereafter, two ducks took up residence in and around the pond in the NGA's sculpture garden. They were instantly christened 'Gough and Margaret'. Subsequently, it was discovered that both ducks were drakes; using the pond as a baptismal fond, they were rechristened 'Gough and Van Gogh'.

The late Bob Collins remembered visiting a Catholic church on Bathurst Island, where the spiritual leader of the Tiwi people asked, 'Are you a pillar of the church, Mr Whitlam?'

'No, Father, I'm more of a flying buttress – I support the institution from the outside.'

John Button famously described the life of a Senator as like being a live-in student at a posh private school. He also complained to me about the waste of his efforts – the not-unfamiliar experience of driving halfway across Victoria to address a meeting that, on his arrival, nobody had bothered to organise.

During one election, the dismal destination for Button was a meatworks outside Sydney. On his arrival there was only one bloke in sight. The notional chairman.

When the Senator enquired as to the whereabouts of the crowd, the chairman revealed that the meatworks' management had refused permission for the meeting. That the employees had immediately called a stop work. That a resolution was moved to the effect that the meeting would be held at noon as arranged. That then, as a protest, the men would stop work for the rest of the day.

Button nodded and asked, once again, for their whereabouts.

It was explained that 'following the moving of a resolution for a stoppage at noon, an amendment was moved that the men could go on strike immediately. It was carried and they all went home.'

Bill Hayden tells the story of hurrying to Parliament House to warn Whitlam of the Kerr conspiracy. It was only a hunch, but a powerful one.

'I said, "Gough, I've got to talk to you," and he came out of the room. This was the conversation, this is what Kerr said. "I'm telling you now, my copper's instinct tells me that this guy is going to sack you. He's thinking of an early election to sort things out." Gough had his spectacles in his hand, and his striped shirt on, as

I remember, and he drew himself up and boomed, "Comrade, he wouldn't have the guts." And he walked back into the room.'

∽

There's a story that Keating was the first to meet the dismissed Whitlam on his return to Parliament House. 'You're sacked!' Whitlam snarled at a shocked Keating.

'What for?' Keating called back. He didn't know that the sacking applied to all of them.

∽

Senator James McClelland – the legendary 'Diamond Jim', to distinguish him from his contemporary Senator Douglas McClelland, who was known as 'Rubber Dougie' – told me a story that he believed really explained the Dismissal. It stars Sir John Kerr, whose feelings for Gough Whitlam at the time apparently approached adoration.

The scene is a private home in Canberra, where Sir John joins Jim and other Labor luminaries for a bit of a piss-up. The GG has driven from Yarralumla in a Mini and parked it on the nature strip. According to Jim, a good time has been had by all, until a somewhat inebriated Kerr says he'd better get back to the office in case Her Majesty rings.

He is heading for the door – and the Mini – when the Labor luminaries block the exit. 'You can't drive, John. You're pissed. You'll finish up ramming the car into a tree.'

'No, I'll be right,' slurred the almost head of state.

But Jim removes the car keys from Kerr's hand and calls a cab. Jim and John then amble together towards the front gate. 'It was a moonlit night,' Jim related to me. 'Quite romantic, really. I recall the soft shadows of leaves on the grass. Halfway to the gate, John stopped, turned to me and said, "Do you like me, Jim?"

'"Of course I like you, John – we've been friends for years."

'"But do you *really* like me?"

'"Yes, I *really* like you."

'"Then give me a kiss."'

Though nonplussed by the request, Jim pulls himself together and provides a peck on the cheek. 'No!' says the GG, puckering up. 'I want a proper one!'

Extrapolating from the yarn, Jim explained to me that, in his view, Kerr fell out of love with Gough and for some reason transferred his affections to Malcolm Fraser. This clearly differs from the views of constitutional lawyers.

In the aftermath of the Dismissal, Whitlam demonised Sir Garfield Barwick as a full member of the putsch. He saw the extracurricular conduct of the High Court judge as verging on the treasonable. Later, at a Canberra golf event, Whitlam was happy to meet the West Indian cricketing hero Sir Garfield Sobers. 'You are one Sir Garfield I *will* shake hands with.'

During the final, fatal election of 1975, the doomed Whitlam rejoiced in attracting the largest crowds ever seen at Labor Party rallies. One was packed with members of the Italian community, amongst Labor's most fanatical supporters.

So rapturous was the applause that one of Gough's private secretaries, John Manter, said, 'One half-expected them to shout "*Il Papa*" or "*Il Duce*".' Manter recalls Italians crowding the leader to shake or kiss his hand.

Flying back to Canberra that evening, Gough held his hand out in front of himself, gazing at it from a number of angles.

'Comrade,' he finally said to Manter, 'I understand what they see in it.'

As chairman of the Australian Film Commission, it was my duty to lead our delegation to the Cannes Film Festival, where we'd try to publicise our productions, get one or two into competition and fight for sales in the 'movie marketplace' – the real point of the annual bunfight. One of our principal competitors was, of course, the British film industry, whose interests in 1987 were represented by the Brad Pitt and Angelina Jolie of the era – Prince Charles and Princess Diana.

As ever, the harbour at Cannes was choked with billionaires' yachts but the HMS *Britannia* outranked them all, with the fuss made about Charles and Di making it impossible for Australia to get noticed. The royal yacht was a powerful reminder of the efficacy of gunboat diplomacy.

The future king and queen of Australia? They were no help to their Antipodean subjects. We looked around desperately for some Australian megastars who might be able to help – and settled on

Gough and Margaret, who were, at that time, in residence at our embassy in Paris. Margaret couldn't make it but Gough flew into Nice airport, where I met him and manoeuvred him into a limo.

He'd arrived on an obscure airline called TATA, which was offering free flights for spouses. Decades later he reminded me of his one-liner on arrival at Nice: 'Free titties on TATA'.

Gough's impact on the Croisette was extraordinary. No sooner had he struggled out of the limo than he was surrounded by paparazzi, who took almost as many photographs of him as they had of Sylvester Stallone the previous day. Not that they'd the foggiest idea who Gough was. But such was his star quality that even the blasé paparazzi were awed by his presence and buzzed around him like blowies.

Somewhere in someone's archives are perhaps the most improbable photographs ever taken of EGW – him posing surrounded by a flock of female bodybuilders in the most abbreviated of bikinis. They flex their considerable biceps whilst Gough smiles down upon them – looking like a parody of Ulysses with the sirens. Finally, the photographers ran out of flashbulbs and Gough began his more official duties for us, hosting a dinner and granting interviews, in which he related his central role in reviving the Australian industry.

Then it was time to return him to Nice airport. En route, he began cross-examining me about the problematic sex life of a mutual friend, a prominent Labor MP. The Leader – as he was accustomed to being called – took a healthy interest in the libidinous activities of Caucus members and was so taken by my vivid description of a particular encounter that he fell off the back seat of the limo. And got wedged between the seats on the floor. It took an immense amount of pulling and tugging to release him. Fortunately, the paparazzi were not around.

Decades after Gough's star turn at Cannes, he reminds me of his 'tit-for-tat' one-liner but fails to remember laughing so hard in the limo that he slid to the floor. He has also repressed the memory of being winched onto the footpath and discovering, at the check-in counter, that he'd lost his TATA ticket.

I can still see him standing in splendid isolation in the departure lounge whilst the lower orders, including myself, rushed around trying to make amends. Gough was not used to lifting a finger. He existed, others organised. It's something that seems to afflict ex-Prime Ministers – a disinclination, even an inability, to deal with the detritus of everyday life.

When Bob Hawke left the Lodge he lost the services of his butler-cum-valet, who'd anticipated his every whim. And Bob had neglected to prepare an exit strategy for himself and Hazel – in the short term they'd nowhere to live. The erstwhile Minister for Tourism, John Brown, offered the Hawkes a spare apartment in Sydney, from which he soon received a plaintive phone call.

'There's nothing in the fridge,' Bob complained.

'Well, you'd better go out and buy something,' suggested John.

'But I've got no money.'

Once again John came to the rescue, while the Hawkes confronted reality and faced an uncertain future.

Reunited with Margaret in Paris, Gough hosted a small dinner in his digs at Harry Seidler's awesome and authoritarian embassy. It's hard to forget Gough wandering around in his underpants as the hour approached. But this startling sight was eclipsed by his behaviour during the meal.

Amongst the few guests were two South Australian politicians who'd been attending a conference on 'dry region agriculture'. Their accounts of the affinities between Australia and Israel failed to amuse Gough and, despite my attempts to buoy him up, he was clearly profoundly bored. So much so that he approached the various courses in the manner of Dr Samuel Johnson – as recorded by his faithful amanuensis, Boswell:

> *His looks seemed riveted to his plate: nor would he, unless when in very high company, say one word, or even pay the least attention to what was said by others, until he had satisfied his appetite, which was so fierce, and indulged with such intenseness, that while in the act of eating, the veins of his forehead swelled, and generally a strong perspiration was visible.*

Gough ate the first course ravenously and then, before the plate was removed, fell asleep. Margaret shook him awake for the second course, which, once again, was enthusiastically masticated prior to a return to unconsciousness. Ditto for the dessert. Then, by earlier arrangement, we grateful guests thanked the Whitlams for their hospitality and headed for the lifts – only to secretly return once the South Australians had hailed a taxi. Only then did Gough wake up, and he spent the rest of the evening regaling us with anecdotes.

For about a year I 'did breakfast' for 2UE, warming the seat for Alan Jones. And when Gough came in for a chat it was necessary to 'do breakfast' literally. To get him to front required an undertaking that bacon and eggs would be provided, which he'd consume before, during and after the on-air chat.

Some years later, seeking to interview him in his office on the thirtieth anniversary of the Dismissal and remembering his gargantuan appetites, I asked my ABC techo to detour for some cakes. When he arrived and unpacked our microphones and cables, he also presented Gough with a cardboard box full of the runniest, custardiest cakes you could imagine.

This prompted the great man's aide-de-camp to scurry into the bathroom and return with a very large towel, which he draped over Gough's shirt as a huge bib. So while Gough attacked Sir John Kerr he also attacked the cakes. The towel was bright red, reminding one of the ruddiness of the Kerr complexion and, at the same time, the long history of bloody revolutions. By the time the interview was complete, the cakes had been consumed and Gough looked like Mount Vesuvius post-eruption, with cream and custard replacing the lava.

In almost every situation with Gough, food came first. And quantity was more important than quality. Many a condemned man has had a hearty meal before being taken to the place of execution, whereas Gough had a hearty meal in his office *after* his execution by Kerr on 11 November 1975. Whilst those around him were urging massive retaliation – at least a phone call to the Queen that might put a stake through the GG's heart – Gough was jabbing at a steak.

On 8 March 1977 Whitlam joined in the welcoming of the Queen to Parliament House. At the reception he made the following speech: 'The Commonwealth is positioned under the Southern Cross rather

than the North Star. Half of its members, republics and monarchies alike, are located in and around the Indian and Pacific oceans. The United Kingdom is now a lonely outpost of the Commonwealth. The United Kingdom! I see some of your subjects there want you to be Queen of Scots. Elizabeth, Queen of Scots, does not sound quite right. Though not as bad as Queen of Queensland. And last week it was proposed that you be Queen of the Solomons. What next? Queen of Sheba?'

A few decades later, a new Labor PM, Paul Keating, had the task of removing the crown of Australia from the Queen's collection. He told me the story of arriving at Balmoral Palace for informal discussions. So informal that the Queen felt it would be appropriate to invite the Keatings to a barbecue. He recalls bouncing around the royal property in a Range Rover driven with considerable panache by HM, and then arriving for a sausage sizzle personally conducted by the Duke of Edinburgh.

The Queen was only vaguely miffed by the prospect of an Australian republic and made no objections to Keating's proposal. The transition would be conducted with dignity and respect for HM's position. Keating would permit no denigration of her great and historic services. Whereupon the Duke began doling out the sausages.

On 1 February 1993 *The Sydney Morning Herald* reported on a flight back to Sydney after the funeral of Sir Paul Hasluck in Perth. It seems that Gough and Bob Hawke were 'the focus of some discreet autograph hunting'.

'Travelling with him on the plane was former Western Australian Senator, and Minister in the second Whitlam Government,

John Wheeldon. Wheeldon leant across to the great man and said, "Comrade, I've been keeping a tally of autograph requests to you and Hawke, and so far it's been going your way by 12 to one."

'"What do you find surprising about that?" boomed Gough. "Think how many there would have been if we were back in economy class."'

◈

Bill Kelty and I cook up a little plot. It's designed to save Western Democracy. Civilisation as we know it. In broad terms, we want to persuade Keating to allow MPs conscience votes pretty much across the board.

It's not only the public who are sick of politics – so are most politicians. Party discipline would be maintained on a short list of issues, but pollies would be free to consult with their electorates and with their personal beliefs before casting a vote on a wide variety of bills.

We've been trying it out on selected heavies in the ALP, and I volunteer to phone Gough Whitlam. Oddly enough, Whitlam and Kelty don't know each other.

Gough was a bit iffy, not to mention butty, about our great idea. His ifs and buts were, however, expressed in a splendid outpouring. Gough didn't draw breath for well over an hour, during which he gave me a guided tour of every nook and cranny in democratic voting systems, with a side trip to the history of referenda. It was a typically bravura performance from the greatest diva in our political opera, from *La Stupenda* of democratic socialism.

Some years ago I was befriended by the then Israeli Ambassador, the dazzlingly intelligent Michael Elizur. Michael admired Gough enormously; he saw him as one of the most formidable figures in modern politics. While smiling at his vanities, Michael was awed by his intellect and, on his return to Tel Aviv, asked me to organise an introduction for his successor, Abraham Kidron.

Kidron had been involved in negotiating the Camp David Accord. Before being sent to Canberra, he'd been Israel's man in Manila. I remember him as being as tall as Whitlam and comparably aristocratic – yet his account of their encounter was full of wonderment. 'He cross-examined me on every detail of Israeli politics and knew more about it than anyone I'd met,' marvelled Kidron. 'He knew the names – in Hebrew – of all the splinter parties. He knew about their beginnings and their fractured coalitions. But then, he also knew everything there was to know about Filipino politics, rattling off the names in Tagalog.'

Nobody who knew Gough would be surprised. Stories, true and apocryphal, abound about his breadth of knowledge. One of my favourites concerns the trip to Australia of Nelson Rockefeller. When Nelson discussed Rockefeller family history, Gough again and again corrected him on matters of detail. And in each case Rockefeller had to concede that Gough was correct.

Let the record show what became of the Kelty–Adams plan.

Our initial assumption was that Parliament came alive – and that parliamentarians were at their best – during a conscience vote. That much of the rest of the time, parliamentary proceedings were arid, dull, predictable and frequently insincere. Members would speak against their personal beliefs on a variety of issues, far too intimidated to express dissent let alone cross the floor. Consequently, voters dismissed them as little more than ventriloquial dolls.

Kelty's idea was that the ALP would encourage independence from its MPs – that only on half a dozen key issues would party discipline be required. Foreign affairs, major financial policy, health and education. But everywhere else the expression of personal views would be encouraged, not just tolerated. We saw this as making a career in politics more interesting, a big improvement from smarting under the lash of the Whip.

But it was not to be. Keating was not alone in shuddering at the prospect. Anyone who attains the prime ministership wants to see his underlings rowing as rhythmically, and in the same direction, as slaves in a galley. Could you imagine, for example, Kevin Rudd permitting even minor variations on his themes? More significantly, even the MPs we sought to liberate seemed frightened of freedom.

As a result, the current federal Parliament contains a total of one Barnaby Joyce.

Kelty, when the diminutive leader of the then-powerful ACTU, came up with the idea of the Whitlam Lectures. We would round up the usual criminals, the icons of the Labor movement and public intelligentsia, to celebrate the leader in addresses that would fill town halls across Australia. I would be the MC and the great man himself would launch the series on 19 November 1997. The setting was one of the most magnificent of our municipal mausoleums – the Sydney Town Hall.

When the great day arrived, the temperatures were through the roof and the air-conditioning wasn't working. So the capacity crowd was close to asphyxiation – and I feared for Whitlam's survival. As

Gough gripped the podium, I sat just a few feet away, watching him sweat and sway. Would the eponymous lecturer die at the podium? But somehow we made the distance.

It was the final lecture in the inaugural series – in Adelaide on 21 April 1998 – that proved more problematic. It was to be given by Don Dunstan under the heading of 'A Vision for a Fair Australia' and we'd booked the Adelaide Town Hall. The tickets sold out in a few hours, so we booked a larger hall, which also immediately filled. So we finished up in a cavernous convention centre. Once again, there was a rush on the box office. Clearly, people realised they'd be witnessing an historical event. Don was fatally ill and Gough was eighty-two. The prospects of solo performances in the future were diminishing – and it was highly improbable that the two of them would ever share a stage again.

Gough flew over from Sydney and John Dawkins, known to his friends as Jim, threw a pre-lecture cocktail party at his Adelaide house, a scaled-down version of *Gone With the Wind*'s Tara. Forever mischievous, Dawkins proceeded to goad Don and Gough into an argument. Already the Whitlam Lecture was fraught with difficulty, thanks to the behaviour of a third prima donna. Roger Woodward, the most charismatic and cantankerous of Australian pianists, had agreed to thump away on the Steinway as a prelude to Don's address – but had thrown a tantrum over the quality of the instrument. All attempts to placate him had failed and the audience would be disappointed. The promised recital would not occur. Roger had left the building.

Meanwhile, back at Tara, Whitlam and Dunstan were going for each other. Never close at the best of times – Dunstan had found it desirable to distance himself from Whitlam during Gough's intensifying crises – the two of them were squabbling over, of all things, railway legislation. You might not consider this a particularly exciting topic, but each was laying claim to major reforms of the railway system – and were doing it so passionately that the lecture faced derailment.

By the time we all arrived at the Convention Centre, Gough and Don weren't talking. As MC, I had not only an abandoned piano but a very huffy Whitlam Lecturer and an even huffier Whitlam, who refused to come on stage and simply sat there glowering. When I finally told this story in an interview for the Don Dunstan Foundation, Whitlam was so enraged that he treated me in the same way he'd treated Don. He refused to talk to me for months on end.

The lesson? Have one prima donna per performance – not three.

About twenty years ago I discovered that Gough Whitlam had ordained a funeral committee for what he clearly believed would be a very grand occasion. Its membership included the ALP's National Secretary, Johno Johnson (then the President of the New South Wales Legislative Council) and various luminaries from the arts and academe. All was revealed to me by a family member who doubles as a musical adviser.

I suspect Gough had been inspired by the funeral of Lord Louis Mountbatten, who died at the hands of the IRA. Mountbatten had been planning his last hoorah for years, apparently storyboarding the event in the way that Alfred Hitchcock did his movies. Right down to such details as having a pair of highly polished boots reversed in the stirrups of a favourite horse. But it was a subsequent royal funeral that enthralled Gough even more. In 1997 Gary Gray, the National Secretary of the ALP, recalled Gough convening an urgent meeting of the committee: 'Gough said, "I've been watching Princess Di's funeral on television and I've had some new ideas."'

At the time of writing, the great event, both long awaited and dreaded, has not occurred. But it would seem that Gough has decided on the setting for the ceremony's climactic moments. Centennial Park. Gough thinks it'll be needed to contain the crowds.

Taking time off from planning his funeral, Gough visits my cluttered home in the middle of Darlinghurst's red-light district. The place is cluttered with the detritus of history, with bric from Rome, brac from Greece and piles of shards from Egypt.

Barry Humphries once suggested that my visitors smear themselves with Vaseline so they could squeeze between the artefacts – and that I should have dressing-gown cords looped from wooden stanchions. Other visitors chose to pretend the place was empty. That had been the response of Patrick McCaughey, who'd been director of the National Gallery of Victoria before moving to the Australian National Gallery. When I asked him why he'd ignored what Humphries called my 'collection of broken rubble' for two solid hours, Patrick confessed that he was 'frightened I might say the wrong thing and make a fool of myself'.

Such a possibility does not occur to Gough, who, on his arrival, proceeds to give me a guided tour of my own collection. 'Etruscan,' he says, pointing an imperious finger. 'Etruscan, not Roman. This? Greek, 600 BC. Egyptian, twenty-fifth dynasty.'

As usual, dammit, he was absolutely right.

At Canberra airport Qantas has what is, effectively, a small private lounge for politicians and upper-echelon apparatchiks. With Parliament in session, it's all but empty. Only Gough and I are waiting for a flight. We must have missed the boarding call because there are suddenly amplified requests for Messrs Whitlam and Adams to join the flight. Gough is as immobile as he was at Nice airport. But this time he hasn't lost his ticket. He wants another kind of assistance.

When a worried Qantas staffer comes over to hurry us along, he demands to know what sort of aircraft will be taking us north. She rushes off and returns with the technical information. A such-and-such jet. Gough remains motionless. 'And what is the aircraft's number?'

'Do you mean the flight number?'

'No, the aircraft's number. It will have one painted on the fuselage.'

Showing mounting consternation – and mystification – the woman disappears and a few seconds later returns with the information. Gough jots it down in a little notebook. Finally he deigns to rise, and with the amplified voice becoming strident we head for the departure lounge.

'What was all that about?' I ask.

'I keep a log,' says Gough. 'I've kept it since the early 1940s. I fill it in after every flight. The aircraft type, its rego number, the destination, the duration and the kilometres flown. I'll fill in the details just before I go to bed tonight.'

I had crossed paths with trainspotters before, but I'd never realised that Gough was a plane spotter.

With Whitlam frequently known as 'the Great Man', Malcolm Fraser had to make do with 'the Big Bloke'. On leaving the prime ministerial office, he overheard a snatch of conversation between Andrew Peacock and his Country Party mate Peter Nixon. Peacock was explaining that he had a new horse which would run in the Melbourne Cup.

'What did you call him?' asked the PM.

'Big Bloke,' said Peacock.

'How's he doing?' said an obviously delighted Fraser

'Well, he was a bloody nuisance at first. It was just about impossible to get him to do anything. Then we found the solution and now he's perfect.'

'What did you do?'

'I had him gelded.'

Jim Leslie, previously the CEO of Mobil and latterly the Chairman of Qantas, headed an outfit called Advance Australia, with a board of the high and the mighty. Fraser gave the board the task of mounting a campaign to persuade Australians to favour local goods over imports and, as Advance Australia was largely my idea, I was kept on as an adviser.

Seeing Fraser's task as daunting, I suggested some market research. The results could hardly have been worse. Group discussions confirmed that Australian products were seen, by and large, as rubbish. When a product had a 'Made in Australia' sticker affixed to its flank, the consumer's response was not patriotism but apprehension. Whereas Japanese goods, once viewed with contempt, had attained a comparable status to those of Germany. This prejudice was particularly potent when it came to automobiles.

Jim and his committee reported to one of Fraser's most power-ful front-benchers, Phillip Lynch. The first Roman Catholic in the Ministry, Lynch was more in awe of the PM than he was of the Pope. 'You'd better tell Malcolm,' he said, making it perfectly clear that *he* wasn't going to tell him.

A meeting was convened in Fraser's office, which was, let it be said, more of a theatrical set, with its flags of Australia and potted plants the size of saplings. The flags wilted and the plants seem to retract like anemones when Fraser returned from a long lunch more than a little pissed. He glared at us and, one by one, our contingent seemed to disappear. Phillip Lynch hid behind one flag whilst Jim Leslie chose another. Within seconds the office seemed to have emptied – except for Malcolm and me, the most junior member of the delegation.

So it fell to me to read the 'executive summary' of the research. Fraser seemed to grow even taller and more threatening as I told him the bad news – and his voice boomed in rage. 'Tell them' – them being the Australian public – 'that the Holden is better than the Mercedes! Tell them that the Falcon is better than the BMW!'

Coming from a Lancia fancier, this outburst of automotive nationalism sounded silly. Yet not a squeak came from Phil, Jim and the rest of them. Unfortunately, I had the floor. 'No, Prime Minister, you tell them. But I'm afraid they won't believe you.'

On the PM's instructions, we went on with the campaign anyway – employing Alex 'Life. Be in it' Stitt to make amusing animations on the transcendental excellence of anything manu-factured in this country. At the time of writing, the almost total absence of a manufacturing industry suggests our campaign was not a wild success.

French security forces are following a Palestinian around Paris – someone deemed to be a potential terrorist. They smash a door down and burst into a shabby hotel room, where they find the Palestinian in bed with a prominent Australian politician. Not that we knew about it at the time. Unlike his own misadventures in Memphis, Fraser had this embarrassment for an 'in the closet' colleague hushed up.

I didn't learn about it until Howard was Prime Minister, when someone seeking to unseat him came and offered me some documentation on the Paris bust. His target was not the hapless participant but the PM. At a time of mounting ministerial scandals, this could be another nail in Howard's coffin.

I looked at my informant incredulously and told him that I wouldn't touch this with a barge pole. I was on the record as defending Don Dunstan against attacks on his sexuality – why on earth would I be party to this? No thanks and no thanks. Peddle it somewhere else. The leading Liberal did. Furiously, he tried to pass it to Mick Young, then to others lower down Labor's food chain. I'm pleased to say that nobody would touch it.

Despite rampant homophobia in the ranks on both sides of the House, being gay remained a private matter. Homosexuality wasn't taboo. To use it as a weapon was. The otherwise admirable Bill Heffernan was the first to break this golden rule when he made allegations about Michael Kirby, who had, of course, outed himself some years before.

Australia has had a couple of gay Prime Ministers. Nobody has outed them. Not even the shock-jocks. Least of all Alan Jones.

These days, the Australian Film Institute Awards – I always preferred to call them the Ozcars – appear to be solid columns of glass or crystal and look as indestructible as bricks. This is in marked contrast to those proffered to winners at the most ostentatious Ozcar ceremony in the AFI's history, which were whimsical wisps of Perspex orbiting each other like the double-helix model of the DNA. Highly spectacular but, as it turned out, foolishly frail.

In 1978 Channel Nine in Perth had opted to stage its telecast in a new complex designed for mega concerts and corporate conventions. The host would be the Premier, Charlie Court. To maximise photo ops for Sir Charles and to give the occasion some celebrity oomph, the AFI had planned a near-death experience by inviting Fred MacMurray and June Haver – though their connections to Australian cinema seemed as frail as the awards. Fred and June would be augmented by two younger celebs – Britt Ekland, once the spouse of Peter Sellers, and the most interesting of the foursome, Brenda Vaccaro, well known in Hollywood for her eccentricities. At the time of her arrival in Perth Ms Vaccaro was crusading against vaginal deodorants, announcing herself as the President of the Society for the Promotion of Natural Body Odors.

As Chair of the both the Australian Film Institute and the Australian Film Commission, I was Ms Ekland's date. As I sat beside her in front row of the amphitheatre, she gave me a running commentary on the male actors' bums.

I was more concerned with politics than posteriors. Most Australian filmmakers had been wholehearted supporters of Gough – some of us had sung in the 'It's Time' chorus. To us, the incumbent PM was the anti-Christ. But we needed to deal with Fraser on film funding – to get him to approve the 10BA tax concessions that had been promised but not delivered. So the last thing I wanted was for the AFI ceremonials to become another anti-Fraser demo. The bloke most likely to use the opportunity to heap abuse on Malcolm was, of course, Bob Ellis . . . and he was up for an Ozcar. Before the ceremony, I had taken him aside and made him promise, Scout's honour and mother's dying oath, to behave himself.

As the evening proceeded, the AFI awards fell to pieces in recipients' hands. Soon the stage was covered with bright, iridescent shards of perspex, the winners returning to their seats with little more than stumps. Britt was enjoying herself – quite a few bums met with her approval. For me, though, the tension was mounting as Bob's turn at the lectern rapidly approached. I kept glaring at him, my murmured threats answered with mumbled reassurances. But as Bob had drunk a lot of Charlie Court's grog at the glittering reception I was unconvinced.

Finally, Bob's name was called and he wobbled up the steps to receive the glittering, disintegrating prize. Britt Ekland was underwhelmed by Bob's bum but the audience tittered appreciatively as he crunched over the perspex litter. Though Bob accepted his award tenderly, it promptly fell apart. As did Bob himself. After thanking everyone in the known universe who'd contributed to his film, he launched, as I'd always known he would, into a nationally televised tirade about the Prime Minister. Fraser was a traitor to democracy, a born-to-rule bully, a political assassin – and Bob was just warming up. With the entire audience frozen in shock, Bob finally drew breath. And vomited all over himself, his disintegrating award and the stage.

$$\backsim$$

When Bill Hayden resigned as Opposition Leader in 1983, he added a new canine to Australia's political vernacular. 'I want to say that I am not convinced the Labor Party could not win under my leadership. I believe a drover's dog could lead the Labor Party to victory, the way the country is.'

Decades later, that dog is at least as famous as the one sitting on the tucker box five miles from Gundagai.

In *The Life of the Party* Barry Cohen recalls the endless debates over which site should be used for the new Parliament House. There were three contenders and the debate was unconstrained by party discipline. One Member made repeated attempts to get the call but, failing to catch the Speaker's eye and exiting in a state of high dudgeon, shouted, 'You can shove it up your arse!'

The response of Jim Cope, a considerable parliamentary wit who'd later be Speaker himself, was instant: 'Mr Speaker, I ask that the Parliament consider the fourth site suggested by the Honourable Member.'

In early 1983 a somewhat beleaguered Malcolm Fraser, deciding to capitalise on Labor's feuding leadership, called an election for 5 March – not realising that his opponent would not be the hapless Bill Hayden (aka the Drover's Dog) but the charismatic Bob Hawke (aka the Silver Bodgie).

The backstage dramas leading to Hawke's sudden ascendency had involved a miserable result for Labor in the Flinders by-election and a growing concern amongst MPs that, whilst Hayden might have a narrow victory, his combination of a lacklustre personality with political conservativeness would not encourage lively government. In other words, it wasn't a question of Hayden failing to win. It was the strong possibility that he would.

Amongst those urging Hayden to step down was Senator John Button, one of the party's most influential members. But he was told to cease and desist – and subsequently promised that he would 'not talk to Hawkey' about the leadership. And John kept his promise. Instead, he would ring me on one phone whilst Hawke rang on another and I'd act as go-between. 'Bob, John says . . .' And, 'John, Bob says . . .'

My only significant contribution to the political discourse during the Fraser years was to make the archaeological discovery that Easter Island was covered with giant Malcolms. The looming, gloomy, grey visages of Australia's Prime Minister, tilting at various angles on perhaps the world's most isolated island, became common currency for cartoonists, and it remains a gross injustice that they didn't pay me royalties.

Then, at the end of Fraser's prime ministerial career, the great grey edifice of his grim visage shed a tear. This seemed as miraculous as having a statue of the Virgin Mary weep, or one of Jesus suddenly produce drops of blood on its outstretched palms.

The occasion was election night and the setting the now-deceased Southern Cross Hotel in Melbourne. When making his speech of concession to Bob Hawke, Malcolm wept. Not copiously. Just that single tear trickling down a marmoreal cheek. And even those of us who rejoiced at his passing watched its poignant progress with some pity.

I was able to express my sympathy personally the very next morning – at a general store equidistant from the main gates of the Botanic Gardens and Malcolm's mother's apartment in South Yarra. Our hands touched as we groped for some Lady Scott toilet tissue.

Malcolm's face had resumed its traditional implacability but, as we wandered briefly in 'the Bots' (as the great gardens are called by locals), we talked about the previous evening.

I suggested to Malcolm that had he managed to excrete a tear earlier in his career, it might have softened his image sufficiently to prolong his prime ministership. Rather wistfully, almost tearfully, he conceded the point. Mind you, his successor wept copiously throughout his term in office, but not enough to wash away the prospects of Paul Keating.

It was Malcolm's tragedy that he masked his emotions, whereas his successor would pour tears all over the public.

It's fascinating to compare Fraser's tears with Hawke's. Malcolm's one and only tear was self-pitying. Whereas Bob's tears – and let's take the example of those he shed at the time of the Tiananmen Square massacre – were not so much for any ostensible suffering as recognition of his own compassion. Malcolm wept for Malcolm. And Bob wept for Bob – not in self-pity, but in celebration of his own sensitivity. I made this observation in a column and Bob's never forgiven me. More on that later.

Back in the Western District, Malcolm becomes embroiled in another scandal – not of Memphis magnitude but one that raises eyebrows in the rural sector. He has a bull sale at Nareen and those attending to bid insist that he's guilty of misleading them. By the simple ruse of having somewhat lower fences around his cattle yards than is usual.

'He did it on purpose,' they complain, 'to make his bulls look bigger.' Buyers complain that, on returning home, they found their purchases seemed smaller. There's talk of court action.

Looking down from his great height, Malcolm says, 'Poppycock.' But, to quote Mandy Rice-Davies, 'he would say that, wouldn't he?'

Malcolm Turnbull told the following story to Annabel Crabb for her *Quarterly Essay* – at a time when Kerry Packer was fantasising about buying the *Times* group and introducing a union-busting plan.

'We had a very funny meeting about it at the Dorchester Hotel, working through all the logistics of getting the paper into the country, printing and distributing it. We had these partners from Linklaters telling us about the provision of these acts and so on, and Kerry was getting frustrated. He eventually said: "Look, I'm driving the truck, right? With all the papers on the fucking back. We're coming off the ramp at the back of the building. There are all these picketers. I beep the horn. They don't get out of the way. So I lean out the window and say, 'Can you please get out of the way?' But they don't get out of the fucking way. So I drive the truck very slowly, and I run one over. What law covers me then?" And this partner from Linklaters, very pale, stammers: "The law of m-m-m-murder!"'

Summing up his views of Australian democracy, Kerry Packer once told me, 'Governments are there to do things for you, not to you.'

~

At the end of each day, Kerry's courtiers would gather outside his office for a drink. To apply the balm of alcohol to the wounds of corporate battle.

David McNicoll would be there, doing his Colonel Blimp impersonation, the same act he'd performed for decades as aide-de-camp to Sir Frank. There'd be the up-and-coming Trevor Kennedy, too bright and ambitious for the constraints of journalism – a bloke who'd be seriously considered to replace Jonathan Shier at the ABC, before accusations against him of financial naughtiness with Rene Rivkin and Graham Richardson.

The Nine Network's version of Jimmy Cagney, the pugnacious Sam Chisholm, who seemed to be tap dancing even while standing still, was almost always in attendance. As was, of course, the Queen of Park Street, HM Ita Buttrose. Lesser mortals were invited from time to time as a treat.

I was there, having just pocketed an ACP cheque for $100 000 – meaning I finally had the budget for *The Getting of Wisdom*, the film version of a Henry Handel Richardson novella, to be directed by my then partner, Bruce Beresford. I'd asked Packer for $10 000. 'I don't deal in ten thousands. I'll give you a hundred grand,' he'd said, 'but I want the TV rights in perpetuity.'

While the courtiers did their best to amuse him, Kerry sat in his corner, in Sir Frank's old possie, sipping his favourite drink. Passiona. He hadn't touched alcohol since his early twenties, when he'd been responsible for a fatal car accident.

McNicoll arrived to tell the gathering he'd been in Canberra that day, signing the D notices on behalf of ACP. The D notices? Australia's counterpart to the Official Secrets Act, a leftover from the Second World War. A list of topics the Australian media agreed not to touch 'for reasons of national security'. Kennedy asked McNicoll whether the Petrovs, the diplomatic duo whose spectacular defection from the Soviet had been so electorally advantageous to Menzies, remained off-limits. Yes, they did.

'That's crap!' said Kennedy. 'We ought to do a *Bully* cover on them.' Bully for *Bulletin*.

At this point, Kerry Francis Bullmore Packer exploded. 'Write one word about them, Kennedy, and your arse will hit the Park Street footpath!'

Stromboli was erupting on the fifth floor. Kennedy was too experienced to respond, so Kerry started raging at everyone else. It was clear the assembled cast were familiar with this sort of escalating tantrum but, nonetheless, the impact was devastating.

And I sat there, enjoying an anthropological detachment.

Just as suddenly, the eruption was over and Packer struggled from his chair. As he swept from the room, he snarled at me, 'Come and have some dinner.'

He chose a nondescript Chinese restaurant in the Cross and, as he poked at some sweet and sour, I decided to take him on. After all, I had his cheque in my pocket. 'Kerry, that was the ugliest performance I've ever seen. Why the hell do you yell at people?'

He put the chopsticks on the table and just sat there. After an extended silence, he said the strangest thing, in the quietest voice. 'Because I don't know how to talk to them.'

Thus began a conversation that would continue long after the restaurant had emptied and the kitchen staff had gone home. Only the owner lingered on. Much of what Kerry had to say was so wistful and apologetic that I soon realised the great hulk had been an abused child. The way he veered from rage to vulnerability was typical of abused kids, irrespective of class.

The evening ended with him cross-examining me on a score of topics, from ancient Egypt to Charles Darwin. It culminated with black holes.

'What are they?'

When I was halfway through a stumbling version of Stephen Hawking's theories, he interrupted. 'That's what I've got inside me.'

'What do you mean?'

'A big black hole.'

Kerry told me that Clyde copped far more abuse from his father than he did. Frank attacked the older brother over everything, including his obesity. And Frank wasn't happy with Clyde's arty friends or cultural interests. He wanted a different life. Then, in his mid-thirties, Clyde staged a mutiny.

It was all over Bob Hawke and the ACTU, who were attacking the oil companies. Sir Frank regarded Hawke as a Communist and ordered that he be banned from TCN. An infuriated Mike Willesee and Clyde both resigned.

Sir Frank immediately cut Clyde out of the will – and Kerry, oft described as 'the idiot younger son', found himself as heir to the family business.

Apart from the elephant guns, the mounted tusks and the huge lounges with cumulus upholstery, Kerry's study was dominated by a screen that gave him a Big Brotherish view of his network. It was there, balancing plates on our knees, that we watched the very first edition of *60 Minutes*.

Neither of us was much impressed. Despite its famous US model, the program was uncertain in style and groping for an approach to its material.

Kerry started emitting pre-eruption grumbles and, before the credits could roll, was on the phone to poor Gerald Stone to give him the sort of review you wouldn't want to keep in your clippings. Some of the criticisms made sense but most were inchoate and unreasonable.

Nonetheless, the program rapidly evolved into the polished commercial product that has delivered everything from pieces of promotional puffery for Tom Cruise to better-than-average observations of Afghanistan by the late Richard Carleton.

In its beginning, the *60 Minutes* on-camera team was made up of George Negus, Ian Leslie and Ray Martin, each of whom got equal pay and equal billing. But within months it was clear that the cheeky, swashbuckling Negus was emerging as the star. He was to *60 Minutes* what Lennon was to the Beatles, with Ray Martin as McCartney and Leslie bringing up the rear on the drums.

Feeling his oats and believing his own publicity, George soon fronted Sam Chisholm with a demand that his equal pay contract be torn up.

As George awaited a response, Sam lifted the phone and called the boss. 'Kerry, this is Sam. As we've been anticipating, Negus is in my office.'

Sam listened for a moment and passed on the message. 'George, Kerry wants to see you at Park Street. He'll meet you in the pub next door.'

Fifty minutes later, the two of them are breasting the bar. George with a beer, Kerry with a lemonade. 'So you reckon you're not getting a fair deal?'

'No, I'm not.'

'Tell you what,' said Packer, picking up a couple of cardboard beer coasters. 'You take one of these and write on the back how much you think you're worth.'

'Why?' asked a puzzled Negus.

'Because I'm going to write what I'm willing to pay you on the back of the other one. Then we'll compare figures.'

Holding the coasters close to their chest, each wrote down a number.

'Now, no looking at either of them. Let's put 'em face down on the bar.'

So they slapped them down, amongst the beer swill.

Whereupon Kerry reached over, picked up George's coaster and looked at the salary demand.

He then picked up his own coaster, slipped them both into his pocket and said, 'That'll be fine.' And left.

George, according to Kerry, would have felt a thrill of victory. 'But I tell you what, those beer coasters saved me a lot of money.'

Not long after his triumphant renegotiation, George phoned me with a request. 'Will you be interviewed for *60 Minutes*?'

'On what?'

'Not on anything in particular. What I want to do is a fake political interview to show how editing can misrepresent an interviewee.'

I agreed, and on my next trip to Sydney asked the taxi driver to take me to Channel Nine.

'Yeah, that's the one owned by Kerry Packer,' the driver said. 'I know Packer very well. As a matter of fact, he's got me on a retainer. He goes up to the Cross a couple of nights a week, hangs out at the Bourbon and Beefsteak. It's a real dive but Kerry likes a bit of the rough stuff, and while he's inside getting on the piss I just sit there at the kerb with the meter running. And when he finally comes out I get him into the back seat, and as often as not he'll chunder everywhere. But what the hell! I clean it out and pocket some really good money.'

I asked how long this arrangement had been in place, and he told me 'two or three years', embroidering the story with lots of circumstantial detail that would have sounded plausible to the untrained ear.

When I clambered out at TCN, I told him, 'I know Packer very well. He hasn't had a drink for twenty years.'

George and I did the fake political interview. For the program segment, he cut it two ways. In one I seemed to be in favour of something or other whilst in the other it was clear that I was totally opposed. There was nothing too tricky about the process – no fine cutting of individual words or phrases, no tricksy shuffling of sentences. Just simple eliminations.

I never saw the results and nor did anyone else. Kerry heard what George was up to in demonstrating some tricks of the trade and demanded that it be cut.

Packer's other star in political interviewing was Mike Willesee. He'd resigned from Channel Nine when Sir Frank told him that Bob Hawke was to be banned from the network and resumed his employment with Kerry as the presenter of *A Current Affair*. But the relationship had remained turbulent and there'd been various comings and goings.

Kerry and I were having dinner in Paddington when Willesee sailed in. These days he's a fundamentalist Catholic who passionately believes in bleeding statues of the Virgin Mary and the miraculous appearance of the stigmata on the palms and feet of Mexican messiahs. But back then he was the tough guy of television, the poker-faced, hard-voiced interrogator who made politicians tremble.

At that stage of his career, Mike had been shopping around. Like Negus at *60 Minutes*, he thought he was worth a lot more money than Kerry had been paying him. And Kerry, it seemed, had lost the negotiations. Mike was moving his program to Seven.

'Come over here,' growled Packer. Mike came. 'You owe me two million.'

'What do you mean?' asked a hostile Mike.

'Because I ran up the bidding with Seven. I didn't want you, but I wanted you to cost them more than they wanted to pay. That's how you finished up with such a silly bloody contract.'

Memories, memories. I'm standing in a cage in Pentridge Prison's notorious H Division. A few feet away, standing in another cage, is Billy 'the Texan' Longley, the enforcer for the Painters and Dockers. A hard man with a soft face, Longley is fifty years old and serving a life sentence for a murder he says he didn't commit. That's why I'm here – he put his case in a letter. On this day Billy and I began a longer, even stranger friendship than I had with Packer.

Thirty years on and I'm sitting in a small lounge room in a little brick house by a railway line. The octogenarian Billy sits beneath a framed photograph of Marilyn Monroe – the famous 'over the grate' shot. He's not too well these days. So he's had to give up ballroom dancing.

By the time we met at Pentridge, Billy already had an impressive CV. He'd belted up a schoolteacher for bullying his little sister. He and his young mates were into sly grog and debt collection for illegal bookies, and he was soon on the receiving end of cops' boots in police stations. Down the track, his house was bombed twice, and he was charged with the murder of his first wife (in what he insists was an accident) and found guilty of manslaughter. On appeal, he'd been acquitted of six counts of 'wounding with intent to kill' or 'causing grievous bodily harm', before being found guilty of receiving money from Australia's biggest armed robbery. But Billy insisted he was in Pentridge for something he didn't do.

I talked to various people involved in the case. Prosecutors, defence, someone close to the judge. 'Well, he mightn't have done that,' was the consensus, 'but it's hardly the Dreyfus case – he did plenty of others.'

Visiting Bill in various jails, I became fascinated by the Painters and Dockers – a union that was home to men on their way to jail and again on their way out. The police quite liked this arrangement, not only because it provided a continuing cash flow in their direction but also because it was good to know where everyone was. The Painters and Dockers became a clearing house for crime and corruption and the dead were many.

By complete coincidence, I was visited at the time by a young journalist, David Richards, who was determined to 'go underground' in the union and report on their racketeering.

This wasn't merely a dangerous project. It was a death wish. I warned David that he'd be killed. Whereupon he pulled up a trouser leg to show the gun holstered at his ankle. He planned to use an empty shipping container as a 'hide' and photograph 'ghosting' – the pay envelopes being handed out to workers who kept rejoining the queue that represented a nonexistent workforce. Graft from the shipping companies.

David wouldn't be talked out of it. But why tell me? Because he wanted the backing of a newspaper. At the time, having been sacked from *The Australian* by Rupert Murdoch, I was writing for *The Age*. I drove straight into town. But halfway in, I changed my mind. I'd had a blue with the editor the previous week. So I drove back to my office and phoned Trevor Kennedy, then boss of Packer's *Bulletin*.

In five minutes flat Trevor agreed to back Richards, introducing him to editor Trevor Sykes. And Richards delivered! He too saw Longley in prison and, in return for an undertaking to push for a retrial (the same request Billy had made of me), he was given loads of dirt.

Richards' first cover story appeared in *The Bulletin* on 11 March 1980. Others followed. This was investigative journalism at its best. Kerry phoned a few times to thank me – sales of *The Bulletin* were soaring and led to growing pressure for a Royal Commission. Frank

Costigan agreed the articles were the trigger. Despite a distinct lack of enthusiasm by the Victorian Government, he was put to work.

Then, in a twist of fate, Costigan turned his attention from the union to Packer, and soon Kerry was caught in his own net. Thus, *The Bulletin*'s stories led to ever-wilder accusations that its publisher was Mr Big in organised crime.

Kerry, the teetotaller who'd threatened to sack *Playboy* editor John Jost for merely hinting that marijuana might be an acceptable recreational drug, was being accused of trafficking heroin! And worse. There would be allegations of his involvement in murder.

Large amounts of money found in the boot of Kerry's car, used for his gambling addiction, were seen by Costigan's inquiry as his returns on drug sales. The allegations got sillier and sillier, with tonnes of leaks from the commission appearing in Fairfax's *National Times*. This would intensify the feuding between the families and, in the long term, make Packer even more determined to buy Fairfax and wreak havoc and revenge.

Trying to explain the booty in the boot, Kerry had talked of his need to 'squirrel money away' for gambling, and was subsequently known by the codename 'Squirrel'. At *The National Times*, Brian Toohey changed animals – Packer became 'the Goanna'.

The revelations and rumours created a vortex that not even Kerry could handle. His reputation was in ruins, his empire imperilled. And his fair-weather friends in politics – from Prime Ministers to Opposition Leaders – deserted him in droves. He would never forgive many of the most prominent. And suddenly a dynasty that had been doling it out for decades was on the receiving end of a media attack.

He spiralled into depression, seeming even to shrink physically. And sitting in his office (with a revolver in the drawer) or in his study (with the elephant guns in the cabinet), he frequently discussed suicide. Then Trevor Kennedy and Malcolm Turnbull talked him out of it and persuaded him to identify himself as 'the Goanna'.

Kerry and I had one of our longest discussions, just the two of us, going through the list of allegations that *The National Times* had printed. Some I knew to be ludicrous but others were troubling. Kerry did his best to deny all charges, to explain them away. And that meant a counter-attack on Costigan and *The National Times*.

And this all started because of my meetings with Billy Longley and David Richards, and the front-page stories in Packer's own magazine.

When Billy Longley finally got out of jail and took up ballroom dancing, he still needed to make a quid. So he returned to a profession he had as a teenager. Debt collection. As Billy told me, things went pretty well. 'I'd just leave my business card in the letterbox. People would always pay up.'

I didn't hear from Billy for a few years. Then an urgent phone call. Through his contacts on the wild side, Billy had heard of a plot to kidnap and perhaps kill Lloyd Williams, one of Packer's partners in the casino business. Williams was in the practice of taking a stretch limo to the Essendon Airport (not Tullamarine), where private jets arrived from Asia. Some of Melbourne's senior crims planned to push Williams into the boot and, if there wasn't a big enough payoff, kill him. Bill wanted to alert the intended victim, not so much out of altruism as in the hope of winning a jackpot.

'Yes, make the call,' I told him.

He did. The plan was averted but all Longley got was a terse acknowledgement.

This should serve to remind our politicians how dangerous the world of whales, high-rollers and glitzy casinos really is. Every few moments outside the Packer's enormous casino on the Yarra, great hellish flames explode. There's a whoosh like you get when a rocket's launched and the surrounding gloom is suddenly fiercely illuminated. The flame should alert those on approach that they're entering a world worthy of Hieronymus Bosch. Family-friendly?

These days, into his eighties, Bill's criminality and connections are all history. Frank Costigan has died but his inquiry lives on – as James Packer's impassioned speech at Kerry's memorial service, apparently written and rehearsed by Alan Jones, attests.

After one of his epic productions, featuring hundreds of humans and at least one elephant, I sent Peter Faiman a fax: 'What's a nice Jewish boy doing directing the Nuremberg Rally?'

Had Hitler known of Peter's skills with spectaculars, he'd have sacked Leni Riefenstahl and signed him for the big torchlight parades. Instead, Sir Frank and Kerry signed Peter up – as, later on, would Rupert Murdoch. And they all used him for their whoppers.

Peter produced and directed the Hogan shows, the Don Lane shows, the Royal Visit concerts, the various awards nights, Australia's Bicentennial telecast (still the largest-scale production in the medium's history) and something monumental in Red Square. I can't remember what it was. Perhaps the Glasnost Gala or the Perestroika Parade?

And he made our most commercially successful film, *Crocodile*

Dundee. To his considerable credit, Peter didn't direct the sequel. He left it to Paul Hogan and John Cornell to destroy their own careers.

Sometimes I'd sit in the control room at Channel Nine and watch Peter put a *Don Lane Show* to air. He'd be calmly watching two dozen screens, murmuring instructions to stars, floor managers, cameramen and musos with all the calm of Napoleon at Austerlitz. The only hint of tension was the fug of smoke from his hundredth Marlboro.

Peter began his career at Channel Nine by choreographing wrestling programs. He'd actually *rehearse* the wrestlers. But finally, exhausted by years of Nuremberging, Peter phoned to tell me that he was on the verge of accepting an offer from Rupert – to help develop Fox News. I phoned Kerry. 'You're going to lose Faiman.'

Despite Peter's decades of loyalty to the dynasty I had to remind Kerry who he was. The response was the telephonic equivalent of a shrug of the shoulders. So I played my best card. My ace. 'Rupert's hiring him.' Instantly, Kerry sprang into action.

Peter was flown to Park Street and asked for an explanation. As paintings of prowling lions and charging elephants gazed down, Peter cowered before Kerry and explained his decision. 'I'm sick of doing the same old spectaculars.'

'I can fix that,' growled Packer.

'I'd like to work on something else, like *60 Minutes*.'

'I can fix that,' growled Packer.

'I'm tired of living in Melbourne – I want to live in Sydney.'

'I can fix that.'

'You've never paid me much money.'

'I can fix that.'

At this point, Peter was losing his resolve.

'Oh, I don't know what to do,' he moaned. 'I could kill myself.'

Whereupon Packer opened a drawer and thumped a large

revolver on the desk. And he said – yes, you've guessed it – 'I can fix that!'

Later, Peter phoned me to say that, despite these fruitful negotiations, he'd decided to fly the coop. He spent many years with Rupert but returned to Nine just in time to produce and direct Kerry's memorial service.

Kerry Packer throws a surprise party for Trevor Kennedy's fiftieth birthday. It's held in a cavernous Chinese restaurant and packed to the rafters with Labor people. Previously the editor of *The Bulletin*, Kennedy is rapidly advancing within the Packer empire and will soon become its CEO. So the party is a 'hot-ticket item', with Hawke and Keating amongst the guests. In a grumbling but good-humoured speech, Kerry confesses that his father would be rolling in his grave to find his son surrounded by so many of the ALP but makes the point that 'Labor politicians are more amusing than the Liberals'.

A number of us do party turns. I follow Paul Hogan and, clutching a teddy bear to remind guests of *Brideshead Revisited*, speak of how Kerry had attended Oxford to do 'a PhD in greed'. There is tension at the table because Hawke and Keating are pitted against each other, as well as the incumbent Bill Hayden, and Keating complains to Kennedy that ACP is on Hawkey's side.

'Wait your turn,' grumbles Packer. Though holding no office in the ALP, his is the voice of God. Keating sits back, simmering. He'll be kept waiting for quite some time.

After a few months in office, Kevin Rudd invited his Labor predecessors to join him for a celebratory din-dins. Sadly, I couldn't attend – I was in Egypt with far less interesting characters like Ramses and Akhenaten. But the goings-on were duly reported.

Together at Kirribilli, the gingerbread cottage of Australian politics, were Bob Hawke, Paul Keating and Gough Whitlam, all with vivid recollections of encounters, incidents and adventures. But Gough tops the tailing of tattle with his account of the brief residence of Jim and Junie. (Though Whitlam refused to talk *to* Jim, he still enjoys talking about him.)

It was John Howard who first drew public attention to the Cairns–Morosi relationship. But the defendants would have been better advised to call Whitlam as a witness in the defamation case Cairns initiated in the Supreme Court of New South Wales. There Cairns denied, on oath, any hanky-panky with Junie.

As Gough told the small gathering, Cairns, as Deputy PM during one of Gough's overseas jaunts, had occupied Kirribilli House with the sultry Junie – rather than the less glamorous Mrs Cairns, Gwen. 'When I got back,' laughed Gough, 'the staff told me that the two of them had been caught *in flagrante delicto* in the garden. Stark, bollocking naked.'

'Tis said that Hawkey was on his best behaviour during his time as Prime Minister – that womanising was 'on hold' and grog forbidden. Yet an extremely beautiful woman who worked for the Premier of Western Australia, Brian Burke, told me of a phone call she'd received from Bob at her desk. 'Do you know who this is?' said a voice, which she had instantly identified.

He'd invited her to dinner – there was some talk of a job in Canberra he wanted to discuss. And for the sake of discretion, he had suggested the dinner take place in his hotel room. I warned she might find herself on the menu and that she should proceed with caution. But she was very flattered – and intensely curious about the job. So she knocked on the door of the Prime Minister's suite.

'He behaved like a perfect gentleman,' she reported back. 'But he didn't get round to mentioning the job. But he's asked me back tonight – for another dinner.'

I was not alone in warning her against accepting this second invitation. The point of no return. She talked to friends in the Hawke retinue – to Bob Hogg, Rod Cameron and, as I recall, David Combe. All echoed my warning. 'Make an excuse.'

So she did, writing the PM a handwritten note to say she'd have to look after her teenage children as one or more of them were ill. Once the letter was despatched, Bob and Rod (and perhaps David) invited her to dine with them.

When they met for the meal an hour later, Bob Hawke walked through the restaurant door. He saw them, joined the table and sat there.

I'd long collected yarns of famous writers who visited Australia in the nineteenth century – the Trollopes, Twains, Melvilles and so on. And there were other literary linkages, such as the letters sent to Charles Dickens by his jackarooing sons in New South Wales. I belted out a column on the subject but came up short, needing another 100 words. So I made up a story. How Leo Tolstoy had fled Russia after a particularly nasty row with his missus and ensconced himself in a hotel in Healesville, Victoria, where he'd had an affair with an Anne Kerin, wife of a local municipal officer and the great-great-grandmother of John Kerin, then the federal Treasurer. I told of how Tolstoy had turned this brief encounter into the great novel *Anna Karenina*.

There was a puzzled response from academics. Experts in Russian literature knew nothing of Tolstoy's time in Australia and demanded hard evidence. So I suggested that they write to John Kerin, who could provide authentication from his family history. And when they did, John did. Doubting Thomases received letters from Canberra on official notepaper. I like to think that in a few decades' time my little fantasy will have become a fact. Or at least a scholarly footnote.

But there's already been an interesting consequence. A few years ago I was launching two books – *Confessions of a Clay Man* and *Notes from the Esplanade* – at Gleebooks. The expatriate Russian author, Igor Gelbach, was born in the Soviet Union during the Second World War.

Introducing Igor, I told my Tolstoy yarn and, to my astonishment, he became quite agitated. Seizing the microphone, he told the audience that he'd read my column whilst living in Moscow and, believing it to be true, had decided that what was good enough for Tolstoy was good enough for him. It was on that basis that he'd chosen Australia for his home.

From 1985, the Science Minister, Barry Jones, led the charge to raise public awareness of greenhouse issues. I did my best to help. But Barry could also rally the assistance of the CSIRO and the Bureau of Meteorology – which led to an invitation to address the Saving the Ozone Layer conference in London in March 1989. There'd be two keynote addresses – one by Barry and the other by an obscure US Senator, Al Gore.

Hawke was hostile to Barry's attendance but finally said he could go – 'at Mrs Thatcher's expense'. Later, it emerged that Prince Charles would be the after-dinner speaker at a small function for the conference's delegation leaders and some senior scientists.

As Barry wrote in his autobiography, *A Thinking Reed*:

I had Al Gore on one side, the Prince's private secretary on the other. Within a few minutes the latter had asked about me and why I was at the conference. He tapped a copy of Prince's speech: 'You have no idea how difficult it was to negotiate for this with the Department of the Environment. It took four days to settle the text for one particular paragraph.'

He went on to inquire of Barry what Australians thought about 'the family'. Barry asked if he meant 'the family as a social unit'.

'Of course not. *The* family – the Royal Family.'

Barry explained that there was no single response – that while there was respect and affection for the Queen, there was much less for the Duke of Edinburgh.

'Why should there be?' Charles's private secretary exploded. 'The man's a hollow shell. There's no one there.'

As the Prince spoke, his private secretary ticked off each para and was clearly relieved when he reached the last page. Then Prince Charles looked up, smiled and said, 'Now I want to add a few words of my own.' Barry remembers his dinner companion moaning, 'Oh my God!'

You could argue for hours about who's been the most conservative federal leader in ALP history. Many today would argue that it was Kevin Rudd, but in the past the accolade was awarded to Kim Beazley. That certainly seems to have been Malcolm Fraser's view. 'I have only one problem with Beazley,' he'd say. 'I can't think of a single issue where he is to the left of me.'

〰

As the disaster of the Howard–Ruddock response to the handful of asylum-seekers trying to reach our shore in leaky boats overwhelms Australian politics and releases decades of pent-up bigotry, Beazley allows himself to be wedged. When he lines up with Howard on the issue, I get an unprecedented number of letters from readers – 10 000 of them – mostly repeating the same sentence: 'I am ashamed to be an Australian.' And while they are not surprised by Howard's strategies, they are appalled by Beazley's acquiescence. They are, quite simply, broken-hearted by Beazley.

Kim and I have a difficult, desultory lunch in Double Bay, where I nag him on the issue of mandatory detention – linking it to the harsh prison sentences being handed out to Indigenous Australians in the Northern Territory and Western Australia. Beazley insists that he'll fix all these things when he wins the job, but to get into power he's going to have to tread carefully.

I complain that he's not treading at all, and that there's more to leading the Labor Party than running an election campaign. A Labor leader has to lead 365 days a year, every year, not just in the few weeks before an election. That unless he inspires the membership – and Labor supporters – the rusted-ons will abandon him. But he can't see it, or won't see it.

〰

In 1995 *Late Night Live* went to Berlin for Christo's wrapping of the Reichstag. The entire building disappeared beneath a silvery membrane. A few yards away, tourists were still souveniring fragments of the Wall. We were there to interview Germany's best and brightest and, in return for some financial help from Foreign Affairs, I had agreed to address a couple of public meetings, where I found myself duty bound to describe the informality of Australia's political life to some nonplussed audiences.

Australian informality seemed to both fascinate and frighten. A Prime Minister who sat in the front of a limo? People saying 'G'day, Bob' or 'G'day, Hawkey'? The idea of German voters addressing Herr Kohl by his first name – 'G'day, Helmut!' – or seeing him deposit his bulk anywhere but the back seat of a Mercedes limo taxed the imagination.

At a Queensland Labor Party do at the Chevron Hotel in Surfers, Bill Hayden proposed a ban on professional boxing. A little later he was equally ardent in his proposal to decriminalise sexual relations between 'consenting adult males'.

The response from Jack Egerton, the rotund party President, has a proud place in ALP history. Grabbing the microphone, he said of Hayden, 'He's bitterly opposed to a bloke getting a punch on the nose but doesn't seem to mind him getting a punch in the bum.' Egerton then called for a division, asking those who supported him to go to one side of the hall while the 'poofters' went to the other.

The American economist Milton Friedman, nemesis of John Maynard Keynes, visited Australia in 1975, when Whitlam was still Prime Minister, and for a second time during the Hawke years.

Friedman addressed a combined meeting of the Caucus

economic and social policy committees in April 1981, urging reduced taxes and flexible wages as an incentive to significant job creation. Barry Jones recalls him causing 'palpable distress' amongst some Labor MPs.

An old friend of mine from my Communist Party days, the ALP Senator Jean Melzer, was, in Barry's memory, the most anguished. 'For the love of Christ,' she implored, 'what about the poor?'

Friedman said, 'I'm afraid that your appeal to Christ is lost on me – I'm Jewish.'

Whereupon Barry interjected, 'So was Christ, at least on his mother's side.'

Bob Hawke's most famous policy speech took place at the Sydney Opera House. He was transported to the venue in a sort of barge. Most of us attending thought the vessel redundant – that Labor's latest Messiah could have strolled across the wavelets. What followed transcended the political. It was a religious event, with Hawkey confidently predicting – indeed promising – that no child would live in poverty after Tuesday fortnight.

It wasn't so much a policy speech as a revival meeting. Both Hawke and I are children of Congregational ministers. Hence, we feel the gravitational pull and power of the pulpit.

Later, we awaited his arrival at the Regent Hotel, a brisk walk from the Opera House. Little clusters of people in conversation. My cluster was the first in Hawke's path when he arrived, and he walked over, grabbed my hands in his (both of them) and looked at me with tears streaming down his cheeks. He was still, clearly, in a state of ecstasy.

∽

As Minister for Science in the Hawke Government, Barry Jones creates a Commission for the Future. He asks me to chair it, and my brief is to open a dialogue between science and the public, to get discussions going on everything from scientific ethics to research priorities. At the time, Barry points out that the future isn't predetermined. It's not like the railroad track crossing the Nullarbor, with the future being unavoidable as it rushes towards us like a diesel loco. No, it's more like shunting yards full of rails, levers and choices.

As Chairman, I seek advice from the best and brightest and am given a dinner by the Australasian Academy of Science in Canberra. A long 'last supper' table is set beneath the flying saucer dome and, to my left and right, members of our scientific pantheon address my question: 'How will the world end – with a bang or a whimper?'

The first scientist to speak is somewhat dismissive of the nuclear threat. Many missiles will blow up in their silos, others will miss their targets. And even though some millions will die, the world – and humanity – will survive.

'The real problem,' says the next scientist, 'is the giant mouse.'

This provokes a murmur of assent but I plead ignorance. 'The giant mouse? What giant mouse?'

Surprised by my ignorance, he talks of a mouse that has recently been produced in a colleague's laboratory – the biggest, strongest mouse the world has ever seen. Understand that we're not talking genetic modification here – that had yet to enter the vocabulary. But by extrapolating from the mouse, the scientist describes a future where human beings, interfering with the glacial majesty of evolution, will render themselves redundant. 'We will produce a human that is taller, stronger, healthier, more intelligent, disease-resistant and capable of living for centuries. We will have no further role. If we're lucky, some of us will be kept on as household pets.'

A third scientist disagrees. The future will not belong to super humans, but to the superhuman gifts of computers – to artificial intelligence. It's much the same scenario but we will lose our prime importance because of the technologies we're busily inventing. 'In a century we'll be as out of date as indigenes in the Brazilian rainforest.'

Other dire predictions follow until, finally, the quietest member of the group says, 'You're all wrong. The problem is what I see in my laboratory every day. What my colleagues around the world are seeing. What our dials are showing.' And he talks about something called the 'greenhouse effect'. 'We will believe the world will be uninhabitable by 2050.'

A long silence follows and then, one by one, his colleagues agree. Yes, the greenhouse effect, first identified in the nineteenth century, has to be the biggest issue of all.

So Barry and I make it the main priority of the Commission for the Future. Which Paddy McGuinness, then editor of the *Fin Review*, denounces as 'the Commission for Bullshit' in an editorial. And thirty years later the McGuinness view still dominates in Her Majesty's Opposition.

The First Lady comes into 2UE to pre-record a program. I love Hazel – as does everyone who knows her. Earthy, honest, good-natured and, thanks to Bob's behaviour, the embodiment of long suffering.

We began the story with her meeting Bob, then things proceeded nicely and chronologically until, to my surprise, she revealed the death of a baby. And dissolved into tears. Though it was one of those moments described in the business as 'good radio', I told the engineer to stop recording. A deep aversion to invading people's privacy is one of the reasons I didn't enjoy commercial broadcasting.

'Don't worry, Hazel, we'll edit this out,' I promised. And we had cups of tea while she composed herself. Then and only then did we proceed.

Imagine my horror – and hers – when the front-page story on the next day's *Daily Telegraph* screams 'Hazel Cries Over Dead Baby'. Far from stopping the recording, as requested, 2UE had sent a dub of the 'good radio' to the tabloid. Quite understandably, Hazel thought I'd betrayed her. I raged at what passed for management at Australia's top 'talk' station that we'd been betrayed. It took a long time before Hazel would trust me again.

We know what to do with dead parrots. You nail them to perches. But what do you do with a semi-deceased politician? What can be done with an ex-Prime or Foreign Minister? Or, for that matter, with a restless chief executive of the ABC? Whilst in the Lodge, Hawkey had recognised the problem with ex-PMs and decided to establish a brand new tradition – perhaps with his own future in mind. Indifferent to infuriating the rank and file – and many on his front bench – Hawke campaigned to have Malcolm Fraser appointed as Secretary-General of the Commonwealth. Sadly, Malcolm didn't get the job, despite being endorsed by quite a few heads of state in Africa – including Robert Mugabe.

So what was Hawke's exit strategy? He confided to close friends that he saw himself as Secretary-General of the United Nations.

And so did Gareth Evans. And, even more amazingly, so did the ABC's David Hill. Not one, not two but three Australian contenders, each convinced that his blend of skills perfectly suited him to one of the planet's prime positions.

It was no use pointing out to Bob that the odds were stacked against him. First of all, the job had never gone to anyone for whom English was the first language. Secondly, Bob's enthusiasm for the state of Israel meant that he'd be blackballed by the Arab states.

David's credentials? Having run the State Rail Authority of New South Wales and then a comparatively obscure public broadcaster seemed to provide inadequate credentials. But that didn't stop David from campaigning energetically. See the next story!

The most plausible of the trio was probably Gareth, but he failed to make it onto the shortlist. But you can't help but admire their chutzpah.

When David Hill heard that I was going to interview Henry Kissinger, he saw it as an ideal opportunity to do some personal lobbying. Trouble was, Kissinger would be in New York – visiting the ABC's studio in the Rockefeller Center. But magically David appeared at 30 Rock on the day, waiting to usher Kissinger into the studio.

Let the record show that, at the time, Hill and I were not on speaking terms. I'd been campaigning to have him removed from office – though, looking back from the other side of the Jonathan Shier incumbency, David's reign represents a golden era. But at the time I thought him a dreadful bully. And on top of that, he'd always wanted to close down Radio National, that seething hotbed of Trotskyites, Stalinists and Pol Pot supporters.

Sitting in my studio in Sydney, I wasn't entirely convinced that Kissinger would actually front. We seemed very down-market for him. But the idea was that we'd discuss his massive new tome, *Diplomacy*. If you whiz through the chapters on Kissinger's own efforts – many of them verging on war crimes – it wasn't a bad book. But I found the idea of the great man actually rocking along to the Rockefeller Center early in the morning improbable.

So I asked New York to keep the studio microphones open so that I could hear Kissinger arrive – if he did arrive. For a while it looked as though he'd be a no-show. I was on air, talking to a couple of American authors about their new book, and found myself stretching and stretching and stretching what had been, at best, a mediocre conversation. Then, at least, I heard a familiar rumbling voice – and David offering an effusive welcome.

So I wound up my chat with the lesser mortals and prepared to talk to Henry. Clearly, the great man hadn't instantly recognised in David the qualities that would make him the ideal leader of the UN – I could hear Henry treating the ABC's chief executive with considerable rudeness. And when he thumped down into his seat and slapped on his headphones, it was obvious to me in Ultimo that he was in a very bad mood. Flattery was called for.

Thus, my introduction of Kissinger went along these lines: 'In the United States of America, there's a deep conviction that you really can go from a log cabin to the White House. But that log cabin has to be in one of the American states – it cannot have been somewhere in Europe. Which is a pity. For otherwise my next guest might have got to the White House in his own right and not as an adviser to Richard Nixon.'

It worked like a charm. By the time Kissinger answered my first question, he was purring. And no sooner were we off air than I could hear him saying to David, 'That's one of the best interviews I've ever had!'

To which David replied, 'Yes, he's a very good friend of mine.'

Our rendered relationship was apparently magically restored.

'I'm going to Australia in a fortnight,' Kissinger continued. 'I want to take him to lunch.' As, indeed, he did. But by the time David got back to Australia, our friendship had once again gone phut.

Howard lost the Liberal leadership after making some ill-advised observations on Asian immigration in a chat with John Laws. In a nation still embarrassed by memories of the White Australia Policy, it was regarded as a major mistake. So began Howard's wilderness years.

Shortly after he came his cropper, I met him at Sydney Airport, in Ansett's private lounge. I was flying to Melbourne and he was heading for Canberra, so the small room was crowded with Liberal MPs. (Their Labor counterparts were next door, in TAA's private lounge.)

It was an extraordinary scene. Howard was being shunned by everyone. He was the Invisible Man. So the two of us found ourselves alone, dangling English Breakfast teabags in our cups. As much out of pity as anything, I told Howard a political truth – that Labor hoped he'd never get the leadership back. 'They're scared of you. They know you're not scared of them and that you could take on Keating. More than anyone else in the Liberal Party, you understand the Labor Party.'

Just before he lost the job for the second time, I recalled that encounter in a column. And so, it emerged, did Howard. Tom Switzer, then the editor of *The Australian*'s op-ed page, asked the PM if he recalled that early-morning conversation in the distant past.

'I do,' Howard said. 'Quite clearly.'

Perhaps he found my words encouraging. If so, I can never forgive myself.

It's the same lounge some years later. Apart from Sir Arvi Parbo and me, the lounge is empty. Bob Hawke, who's come and gone from the Lodge, enters and spots me. He is instantly enraged. He comes over and, towering above me (towering above people isn't something that Bob could usually manage, but I was lounging in a very low chair), starts screaming abuse at me. It seems that years of loathing have been building up in him and are finally exploding. I try to struggle aloft and it gets mildly physical. Much to the astonishment and amusement of Sir Arvi.

Others arrive and the altercation splutters and sputters out, and we're soon called for our separate flights. I try to work out what detonated Hawke's tantrum and recall that, the night before, I'd made a brief appearance in a TV news story about Bob. The media were hounding him about his involvement with international gambling and allegations about a jockey's misconduct in Hong Kong. A crew had called me for a comment and I'd simply said, 'Bob Hawke has always stood up for the little bloke, in this case the jockey.' That had clearly been the last straw.

British Labour Prime Minister Clement Attlee was regarded as a modest man. In *The End of Certainty*, Paul Kelly recalls Winston Churchill's observation that 'he had much to be modest about'. Paul then goes on to recall an unidentified ALP wit quipping that the Hawke–Keating struggle for the prime ministership was 'a contest between an egomaniac and a megalomaniac'.

The great British radical Tony Benn (in a previous life a viscount) once told me that every politician, irrespective of era, country or political system, came in one of three categories. They were straight men, fixers or 'maddies'. It's pretty easy to allocate leaders accordingly. Thatcher, Reagan, Doc Evatt, Kennett, Keating, Bjelke-Petersen, George W. Bush and Ceauşescu were typical maddies. Neville Wran, Bob Hawke, Bill Clinton, Mikhail Gorbachev and Harold Macmillan were archetypal fixers. And straight men also abounded – the likes of John Cain, John Major, Ben Chifley, Harold Holt, Nick Greiner and Dwight Eisenhower.

There are significant, even great politicians in each category but, far and away, it's the maddies who are the movers and shakers. For good or ill, they change history. Explaining Benn's hypothesis in a column, I cited Beazley as a standout straight man, Hawke as a fixer par excellence and Keating as the very model of a maddie. The next morning Paul rang the farm from the Lodge and I expected an earful.

Anything but. 'It's your mad mate here,' he said, positively purring.

Keating regarded the designation as an accolade, not a criticism. He acknowledged that the maddies were the ones who used power powerfully – who, recognising its enervescence, used every waking moment in its exercise.

I get solid evidence of Keating's creative madness when he phones a few weeks later and says, 'Those mad cunts in the High Court have come down with a Mabo decision. They've chucked it out the door and slammed it on me. Now I'm stuck with it.'

What the court has done, of course, is thrust greatness upon Keating, who, having been forced to pick the Mabo decision, makes it his personal crusade.

Lowitja O'Donoghue later told me that the Aboriginal negotiators were awed by Keating's performance in the long-running and tough negotiations – by his grasp of the issues and his determination to get a result. I was reminded of the great emancipator, Abraham Lincoln, who did not go into the Civil War to free the slaves but to keep the states united. Neither Keating nor Hawke was particularly concerned with Indigenous issues, but when presented with the High Court's *fait accompli,* Keating's conspicuous skills and gallantry came into play. In historical terms, the High Court did the right thing for the blackfellas – and for Keating.

Edna Carew's book on Keating, published in 1988, lists the Opposition's collection of terms Paul used when referring to them in Parliament.

Harlots, sleazebags, frauds, immoral cheats, cheats, blackguards, pigs, mugs, clowns, boxheads, criminal intellects, criminals, corporate crooks, friends of tax cheats, brain-damaged, loopy crims, stupid foul-mouthed grub, piece of criminal garbage, dullards, stupid, mindless, alleycat, bunyip aristocracy, clot, fop, gigolo, harebrained hillbilly, malcontent, mealy-mouthed, ninny, rustbucket, scumbag, scum, sucker, thug, dimwits, dummies, a swill, a pigsty, liberal muck, vile constituency, fools and incompetents, rip-off merchants, perfumed gigolos, gutless spew, glib rubbish, tripe and drivel, thugs of Australian politics, constitutional vandals, stunned mullets, half-baked crim, insane stupidities, champion liar, ghouls of the National Party and barnyard bullies.

By the end of his second term as Prime Minister, that *Roget's Thesaurus* of insults would be ten times the length and far more inventive.

~

At a COAG meeting in the mid-1990s, Prime Minister Keating returned to the conference room at the end of a particularly fractious day to distribute copies of the draft communiqué. All eyes turned to the document.

Suddenly Jeff Kennett rose in his place, stabbing at a particular paragraph, and said, 'This is a lie!'

Keating shot back, 'No, it's a draft lie.'

~

I'm raising an orphan joey at the farm. Bottle-feeding, letting it use an old black skivvy as a pouch. Convinced I'm its mother, it climbs into the shower with me, and jumps into the swimming pool. And it sits beside me on the front seat of the car when I drive to Sydney. At night, it hops around the studio at 2UE and, from to time, rolls into the black skivvy and sleeps on the desk beside the microphone.

There's a visiting delegation of Chinese filmmakers – the so-called 'fifth generation'. I'd met most of them in Beijing and Xi'an and helped organise a welcoming ceremony. And my joey came along. The Chinese delegation is enchanted by it and takes turns sitting it on their laps. Then Keating arrives for a photo op. Surrounded by the beaming filmmakers, he gives it a cuddle as a photographer says 'cheese', a term entirely meaningless to the Chinese. And at that exact moment, the joey pees all over Keating's Zegna suit.

Learning nothing from this incident, the Minister for Tourism, John Brown, cuddles a koala at a similar event – and it famously drenches him in urine. I can't help but remember a marvellous story of when Sir Thomas Beecham was rehearsing *Aida*. Whilst his diva was behaving badly, a trained elephant turned around and, with its back to the audience, pooped all over the stage. Sir Thomas laid down his baton and said, 'Terrible stage manners, but what a critic.'

For a few years I was Chairman of the National Australia Day Council, notionally in charge of cheering things up on Australia Day. For us, the big event was announcing the Australian of the Year. We'd come up with the name in holy enclave but went no further than emitting a puff of white smoke. It was the incumbent Prime Minister's task to name the name. This was usually done in a tent erected on the lawns of Admiralty House, the GG's official Sydney residence, right next door to Kirribilli House, the PM's. Admiralty House is, far and away, the posher of the two, with lawns sweeping down to the harbour. Whereas Kirribilli's garden is a series of scenic-railway hills, voluptuous and quite dangerous curves that had once been the perfect place for nude frolicking by Jim and Junie.

The sequence of events went like this. I'd go to Kirribilli House, collect the PM and Mrs PM, and we'd go next door to identify that year's emblematic Australian.

As a warm-up to what I knew would be Keating's inspiring words, I tried to amuse the distinguished guests with some of the Keating jokes included in our thick Penguin collection. They were, as you might expect, somewhat irreverent, and whilst the audience found them hilarious, Paul smiled tightly.

Annita? She looked increasingly furious. All the more so when I explained that our scholarly researches had revealed that the Keating jokes had started their life as anti-Hitler jokes – and that the two comedians who'd devised them ended up in Dachau. I was trying to make a point about Australia's political freedoms but it was lost on Annita. I felt the chill for the rest of the day.

After the ceremony, I wandered down the lawns with two Pauls – Keating and Kelly. So as to escape the camera crews, we walked as far as we could, until we teetered on a cliff edge. Whilst gossiping amiably, we noticed that the crews were filming us with their telephoto lenses, whilst the sound men were aiming their long-range microphones at us, trying to pick up our words.

So as to guarantee they'd never be broadcast, I suddenly said to Kelly, as if responding to a revelation, 'Really? Rupert Murdoch is gay?'

The then editor-in-chief of *The Australian* paled visibly and all but fell off the cliff. The story didn't go to air but I've no doubt that the footage survives in one of those archives for unbroadcastable outtakes.

Don Watson calls with a question from Keating: would I like to be the Chairman of the proposed National Museum? Being in charge, with the responsibility of creating Canberra's missing link – an institution to join the High Court, the National Library and the National Archives – is, of course, very attractive. Don warns me that money would be tight and that Keating doesn't want to see some profligate and vainglorious monument to the problematic notion of national identity.

I remember us talking about the possibility of using the physical museum as the basis of a virtual museum. As well as a building of substance, if not magnificence, I talk about the possibility of a virtual Smithsonian, linking the National Library, the Art Gallery, the Portrait Gallery and the other jewels in Canberra's crown, using technologies that are already making the Louvre, the Uffizi and the Brit globally accessible.

So we do a deal. I'll be appointed to the board of the hypothetical museum immediately and, after the election, be promoted.

I see the appointment as my last hurrah, the final page in what passes for my public life, and can't wait. But, of course, it was never to be. Shortly after Howard's victory I resign from the board, as I do from my other government jobs, recognising that the future of any organisation with Adams as a board member will be problematic.

Even without me the new museum remains controversial and the culture wars rage around it. As they had about the National Australia Day Council, which I'd been asked to take over when it was on its last legs.

Apart from trying to whip Australians into a frenzy for 26 January, we oversaw the doings of the state Australia Day Councils, which, over the years, had been stacked to the rafters with conservatives devoted to the Union Jack and Her Majesty. So I saw my first duty as having a quiet purge.

The most amusing part of the job, however, was to anoint the Australian of the Year. The board, including such luminaries as Lowitja O'Donoghue, would meet at my place and we'd debate an endless list of nominees. And despite the leftover conservatives on the NADC, Lowitja and I managed to steer the title in a somewhat different direction. Our first appointee – heralded by a puff of white smoke from Paddington – was Mandawuy Yunupingu, whose brother Galarrwuy was a previous recipient.

When Keating made the announcement at Admiralty House, Alan Jones went ballistic. Not .22 ballistic but more of the canon's roar. Never a great respecter of Indigenous Australia, he'd notoriously derided Kath Walker's adoption of her Aboriginal name – Oodgeroo Noonuccal – on 2UE by his sing-song chanting of it. So his fury over Mandawuy was to be expected, though its intensity was startling. So bigoted were Alan's tirades that even his friends at the *Daily Telegraph* were moved to admonish him in an editorial.

So I made one of the criteria for an Australian of the Year 'that he or she should infuriate Alan Jones'. Mind you, whoever we chose enraged the shock-jocks. When I described Stan Zemanek as having the 'brain of a Surprise pea – prior to immersion', his switchboard glowed with protests from loyal listeners. This moved me to apologies – to the Surprise peas. Zemanek's response to Arthur Boyd was as aggressive as Alan's to Mandawuy. 'Who the hell is Arthur Boyd? What's he ever done for Australia?'

So I left the NADC with some regret – and aware that Howard would stack its board as resolutely as he would the ABC's.

⁊

Radio National conducts a poll of listeners. Nominate your favourite speech of all time. It can be historical, contemporary or literary. Thousands of entries arrive, extolling the virtues of the Gettysburg Address or Mark Antony's speech over the body of the slain Caesar. Elizabeth I tells her troops that she may only have a body of a woman but watch out! Churchill tells England they will fight Hitler in the air and on the beaches.

Finally, a distinguished panel chooses its finalists and I ring Paul Keating to congratulate him. 'Do you want the good news or the bad news?'

'The bad news.' Paul's come to expect that.

'Well, you came second in the great speeches of all time contest. For the speech at Redfern.'

'And the good news?'

'You came second to Jesus Christ. The Sermon on the Mount.'

Paul is pleased. He points out that at least 'we're both Roman Catholics'.

Annita Keating tells an extraordinary story to *The Bulletin*. John Lyons gets a scoop with 'I knew our marriage was at an end. Paul told me so over dinner.' Devastated by the story, Paul phones me to protest its untruth. Annita also complains that she'd been written out of Don Watson's book on the Keating prime ministership.

I know Annita's stories of being divorced over dinner and dumped from Don's book are unfair. Don has told me that Annita spent a great deal of money on lawyers, who insisted that most references to her be removed. And the other guests at the dinner during which Paul had allegedly cast Annita into the outer darkness have a very different version of who'd said what to whom.

Paul had been lovingly restoring St Kevin's, a home in Queen Street, Woollahra, previously owned by Leo Schofield. I'd considered buying the place when I moved to Sydney but it seemed too gloomy, even for my melancholy tastes. Paul loved it, however, and spent a great deal of time and money preparing it for his post-prime ministerial accommodations.

Annita had grown used to the luxuries of the Lodge and Kirribilli House and told the other dinner guests, banker David Morgan and former MP Ros Kelly, that she didn't like St Kevin's and wouldn't move in 'without a butler and a cook'. By this stage, Ros was doing quite well in business and David was CEO of Westpac, yet they made it clear that even they couldn't afford such expensive domestic staff. But Annita repeated that without a butler and a cook she wouldn't step through the door.

From that point the dinner was doomed. Paul was devastated but Annita immovable. Morosely, he made the sad observation that her stance would put a lot of strain on their marriage.

Keating and Watson had fallen out over *Recollections of a Bleeding Heart*. Keating regarded Watson's book as both a personal betrayal by Watson and a misrepresentation of his years in office. Once united, the two were completely estranged. In the hope of building a bridge, I suggest to Don that he publicly back Paul on the issue of Annita being 'written out' of the text – by stating that, far from being ignored, she herself had demanded extensive cuts. 'If I got a journo to ring you, would you confirm this?' I ask.

Don says he will – and does when I arrange the call. But Paul spurns the olive branch.

Until he writes his own book, Watson's will remain pretty

much the 'official record' of the Keating years – yet the subject insists that it's wrong on both substantive issues and in its depiction of him (my words) as being as indecisive and gloomy as Hamlet on the battlements of Elsinore. Keating also believes that Watson's account of their time together is self-aggrandising. 'I was in public life for twenty years without Don Watson and did pretty well.'

Paul insists he had no idea what sort of book Don was writing – that he'd abused the access that Keating had given him both as a speechwriter and a close adviser. Don sees it differently, telling me he kept the boss fully informed.

Watson's book was the final blow for Keating. First of all, he'd lost the election. Second, he'd lost it to John Howard – the person in public life he most despised. (I don't think he'd have minded anywhere near as much losing to John Hewson, for whom he had respect.) Third, Paul *really* lost the election – by a catastrophic margin. Fourth, the ALP turned its back on him and tried to write him out of its history. Fifth, and worst of all, he lost Annita. Sixth, the book. It took some time for Paul to recover . . . and to come roaring back into public life.

Finally returning to the fray, Keating begins to attack his long list of enemies. Sometimes he's hurt in the blow back. Over a cuppa, we examine his latest controversy and he acknowledges that he's 'copped a lot of flak'. Whereupon he jumps to his feet and mimes hammering a nail into the wall. 'I go "Bang, bang, bang! Bang! Bang!" And I might hit my bloody thumb. But at least the bloody nail's in the bloody wall!'

∽

Paul's anger over Don Watson's book has spurred him to action from time to time. But a fire in a suburban garage destroyed many of his papers. He's spent recent years trawling through press clippings, sifting and organising them, and to my knowledge has brushed off a dozen offers from publishers. Of course, the book Paul has in mind will be like Freudenberg's *A Certain Grandeur* on the Whitlam years. Technical, self-defensive and light on anecdotes.

That's not the book I want him to write. I want him to tell us of his experience of standing beside Margaret Thatcher at Brezhnev's funeral, of being at the Queen's sausage sizzle, of his surreal encounter with the odious Robert Maxwell. The legislation is one thing. But the life is another.

Mark Latham holds his policy launch for the 2004 elections beneath the great dome of the Brisbane City Hall. Whitlam makes a grand entrance and gets his usual standing ovation, but Keating is smuggled in via a side door.

A devastated Keating phones me later to describe the humiliation. 'The cameras were under instructions to avoid me, and during the edited version that went to air I was edited out.' Keating says that is the end of it, as far as he's concerned. He will never again attend a Labor function.

This reminded me of photographs of Soviet leaders reviewing the troops on May Day from the top of Lenin's tomb. One by one they were written out of history and were airbrushed from the photographic record. Keating, too, was 'whited out'.

As far as the rank and file are concerned, however, Keating is still a hero, as great a star as Whitlam. His shameful treatment at Latham's policy launch is corrected by John Faulkner, who's given the task of organising Rudd's policy speech at the Brisbane Town Hall for the 2007 elections. Once again, the city's municipal counterpart to St Peter's is filled with the faithful and the prayerful. Can Rudd beat Howard?

Keating forms a holy trinity with Whitlam and Hawke for photographers. Whitlam, the straight man. Hawke, the fixer. Keating, the maddie. Rudd? Not a fixer – which is why the fixers fixed him. In the end, a straight man. But in bringing Keating back from the political dead, he fixed a serious problem.

An absence of political madness can be a problem. When Howard defeated Keating, Beazley got the leadership. I visited Kim in Canberra to wish him well. I found the Bomber sprawled on a couch, looking physically enormous but psychologically shrunken.

'I'm sick of death,' he said.

My response is silence. What's this about?

'I've just come back from Port Arthur,' he said. 'Death, so much death.'

Another silence.

'And I've spent a week sitting with Mick Young as he died,' he continued after a while. 'Death again.' A deep breath, then he went on. 'The election loss was another death. Not just a defeat, a death.'

The silence stretches again.

And then the gloomy, despondent man says, 'Paul Keating was a great Prime Minister. I'll never be a great Prime Minister.'

The wan, weak utterance obliges me to reach over and pat Kim on the knee. But his bleak view of his own abilities disturbs me. Such a self-assessment would be unimaginable in a Whitlam, a Hawke or a Keating. Or, for that matter, in a Fraser or a Howard.

When I reported Kim's words to Graham Freudenberg, speech-writer to every Labor leader since Calwell, he made a somewhat bemused observation. 'You realise what this means – that for the first time in a long time we've a sane leader.'

Sane, perhaps, but one of Tony Benn's straight men.

Over the years *Late Night Live* has had some distinguished correspondents in Washington. From within the beltway we'd Clinton's spindoctor Sidney Blumenthal and the pre-Iraq incarnation of Christopher Hitchens. Then came David Brooks, the rising star of the Republican opinionista, and, for the last ten years, the progressive Bruce Shapiro.

Their Canberra counterparts have included Alan Ramsey, Paul Bongiorno, Geoff Kitney, Mike Seccombe, Fran Kelly, Laura Tingle and Christian Kerr, with perhaps the most memorable contributions coming from the wild woman of the Press Gallery, Margo Kingston.

None of your cool detachment for our Margo. Her approach to Australian politics is as passionate and personal as any of the politicians she observes. Case in point: Margo's response to the Hanson phenomenon. Not just to the politics of Hansonism, but to the perils and personality of Pauline.

Margo's on-air performances were invariably unpredictable and sometimes dangerous – to herself even more than to the program. A simple question would be followed by long silences and then an explosion of words, often rendered inchoate because of the emotions that drove them. This was particularly true during the doomed 1998 election campaign, in which Margo followed Hanson on the trail. The title Margo chose for the book she subsequently wrote referred as much to herself as to the candidate – *Off the Rails*.

From time to time on air, I'd suggest that Margo had effectively fallen in love with Pauline, that her fascination with the most eccentric and divisive politician in Australian history – a true maddie – had become obsessive. Whilst Margo was never persuaded by Hanson's politics, she was, it seemed to me, infatuated by the woman. There's no doubt that Kingston put her career on the line with Hanson and was seen to have crossed into partiality.

But that doesn't diminish, for a nanosecond, the value of *Off the Rails*. It's a book without precedent in Australian political commentary, the sort of passionate encounter that makes Bob Ellis's political writing seem reticent by comparison.

Hanson gave Kingston a potted autobiography. 'Being reared in the shop and seeing mum and dad work the hours they did – my father, for 25 years he had that shop (Jack's Café in Woolloongabba, South Brisbane) and he worked 106 hours a week. It was one of the best-known shops, and dad was really well known. We grew up there, and by the time we were old enough we used to peel the onions on the weekend, or we had our jobs – mop the floor or do the spuds or make the chips or we were in there serving. So from the age of 12, every Saturday morning for two years I worked on the counter in the shop . . . I left school when I was 15 and I got a job at Drug Houses of Australia, clerical work, and you got paid $16.40 for the week . . . So I'd work from 8 to 5 o'clock at my day job, and then I'd come home and change and I'd start in the shop, waitress on the tables from 6 and get to bed about 12 o'clock . . . I'd get $5 for the night, but then I'd walk up the stairs and there's mum in bed waiting for the board. That was my board money – so dad would pay me in one hand, and I'd walk up and give mum the $5 for the board. But it made you respect money. It made you realise that you don't get anything for nothing.'

Kingston wondered whether Hanson's ingrained work ethic 'helped explain her resentment against single mothers getting supporting parent benefits and Aborigines getting extra help'.

'Hansonites were a bunch of hare-brained amateurs without cash, talent or experience,' recalled Kingston. 'Surrounded by a marauding media – I almost felt sorry for her.' She instanced 'Hanson's main man, David Oldfield, the only person in the party with a political brain'. Describing him as 'overtly contemptuous of his leader to journalists [and] oblivious to the damage he caused to the image of the woman he called "the product"'. Hanson told Kingston that she didn't like being seen with him 'because some people thought she was a puppet, and she wasn't'.

Hanson surprised Kingston by stressing that she liked Paul Keating. 'Yes, I do. He's strong.' Margo wasn't alone in doing a double-take, one of many during the campaign. Paul Keating – the demonised king of political correctness who, according to the Right, had propelled Australia into all this division and pain on race and multiculturalism – was admired by the woman who'd led the backlash.

It was as surprising as Keating confessing his regard for Jeff Kennett. One maddie saluting another. 'He's the only one of the Premiers worth feeding,' Paul once told me. And in that case, the feelings seemed entirely mutual. Kennett and I discussed Keating on a couple of occasions; after Paul's departure from official public life, Kennett entertained my suggestion that he offer him a job. After all, nobody else did – or would. Until Rudd's arrival, subsequent Labor leaders saw Keating as dead dangerous. They'd cross the road to avoid him, making the sign of the cross.

Kingston's observations about David Oldfield were as compelling as those about Hanson herself. She described his secret work for Hanson, his masterminding of the formation of One Nation – along with a unique party structure that would entrench his growing power.

'Oldfield's most obvious characteristic was his need to construct and display a notorious public sexual persona, despite his constant critique of media interest in Hanson's, and indeed his own, personal life . . . He professed himself addicted to young blondes, admitting to using telephone dating services around the country, and told anyone who'd listen that his perfect woman was a cross between Jayne Mansfield and his mother. "Women find me extremely attractive," he'd tell female journalists . . . Before the election, knowing he was being photographed, he'd put his hand up the skirt of a Sydney date and seemed pleased that the photo appeared in the *Daily Telegraph*.'

Shortly after her election to Parliament, Hanson published *The Truth*, a book claiming that Aboriginal women ate their babies and that tribes cannibalised their neighbours. She defended intense criticism by explaining the allegations of cannibalism demonstrated 'the savagery of Aboriginal society'.

David Ettridge agreed. 'The suggestion that we should be feeling some concern for modern day Aborigines for suffering in the past is balanced a bit by the alternative view of whether you can feel sympathy for people who eat their babies.'

The book also suggested that in 2050 Australia would have a president called Poona Li Hung and that she'd be part-Chinese, part-Indian and 'part machine'.

In November 1997 Oldfield suggested to Hanson that she record a video to be screened to One Nation members and supporters in what was seen as the highly likely event of her assassination. She began her twelve-minute tape – surely one of the most interesting artefacts in the history of Australian politics – with the following message:

> *Fellow Australians, if you are seeing me now, it means I have been murdered. Do not let my passing distract you for even a moment . . . For the sake of our children and our children's children, you must fight on . . . We must go forward together as Australians. Our country is at stake.*

So, it seemed, was a great deal of money. Unwise in her choice of advisers – along with Oldfield she'd heavily relied on the highly colourful John Pasquarelli and professional fundraiser David Old-field – she also became involved in legal disputes amongst her supporters. In August 2003 a jury convicted Hanson and Ettridge of electoral fraud by the District Court of Queensland, and Pauline was sentenced to three years' imprisonment. With her party's regis-tration deemed unlawful, her collection of electoral funding worth half a million dollars led to further convictions.

Hanson's reaction to the verdict? 'Rubbish, I'm not guilty. It's a joke.'

Liberal MP Bronwyn Bishop compared Hanson's conviction with Robert Mugabe's treatment of the Zimbabwean Opposition and declared her a political prisoner. In November 2003 the convictions of Hanson and Ettridge were quashed by the Queensland Court of Appeal – and it was revealed that Tony Abbott had arranged for the lawyers who had instituted the legal action to act on a largely pro bono basis. A *Four Corners* investigation revealed that Abbott had financed a cranky ex-One Nation member, Terry Sharples, in a court case against Hanson. The motivation was deemed to be Abbott's desire to derail One Nation – which seemed singularly ungrateful, given that the Liberal Party had been a clear beneficiary of the Hanson phenomenon.

Facing bankruptcy, Hanson appealed to the faithful for funds, brushing aside the objections of one supporter, who said, 'She can afford to live in a $700 000 mansion just outside of Rosewood. The people up here that she's asking to give money to her are pensioners and farmers that are doing it tough.'

After various unsuccessful attempts to be elected to a variety of parliaments, Hanson joined the cast of *Dancing With the Stars* on the Seven Network. Here, at least, she attracted some votes. Enough to make it to the final.

Let we forget . . .

I come here not as a polished politician but as a woman who has had her fair share of life's knocks. My view on issues is based on commonsense, and my experience as a mother of four children, as a sole parent, and as a businesswoman running a fish and chip shop . . .

I do not believe that the colour of one's skin determines whether you are disadvantaged . . .

I was born here, and so were my parents and children . . . I draw the line when told I must pay and continue paying for something that happened over 200 years ago. Like most Australians, I worked for my land; no-one gave it to me . . .

If politicians continue to promote separatism in Australia, they should not continue to hold their seats in this parliament. They are not truly representative of all Australians, and I call on the people to throw them out . . .

I may only be 'a fish and chip shop lady', but some of these economists need to get their heads out of the textbooks and get a job in the real world. I would not even let one of them handle my grocery shopping . . .

I believe we are in danger of being swamped by Asians . . .

We're bringing people from South Africa at the moment. There's a huge amount coming to Australia, who have diseases, they've got AIDS . . .

❧

John Faulkner and I have nagged the ABC for years to do a life of Keating. During the Howard regime they ran a mile, but lately there have been a few discussions. Often the problem is Paul himself. He passionately wants to tell his story and yet, again and again, seems overwhelmed by reticence.

Even the most mediocre US President finishes up with a presidential library. Jokes about the George W. Bush effort – that it will contain, at most, one book – will not prevent the project going ahead, to join the monuments to such predecessors as Nixon and Reagan. In Australia, prime ministerial libraries are few and far between, though Bob Hawke has been honoured with one at the University of South Australia.

But for Keating? So far, nothing. I beg the State Library of New South Wales to create one for Paul and they make him an offer. Which, characteristically, Keating considers and declines.

Wherever it finishes up and whatever form it takes, there is one thing that must be done. Someone must sit down with Paul – not necessarily on screen but just there to keep things moving – while he pours out a great stream of consciousness. On countless occasions he's turned up at my house and simply started talking – and it's been an astonishing experience. At once revelatory, outrageous and hilarious. Ten, twenty, thirty hours of taping should do it.

The ABC simply must regard this as a central obligation. Failing that, the National Library should be funded so that they can upgrade from audio tapes to video. And let's do it for all the pollies of consequence. It's too late for John Gorton, for Bill McMahon. But there's still time for more hours from Whitlam, and for Malcolm Fraser to tell his story, as he sees it. The evolution of someone who was inspired by the quasi-fascist Ayn Rand to become one of Australia's greatest left-wingers, at least on issues like race and refugees.

Otherwise all we are left with are fragments, scraps, a few feet of film. And anecdotes in collections like this.

In politics rumours spread more rapidly than influenza. When visiting Sydney I invariably stayed at the Sebel Townhouse, the preferred hotel for the entertainment industry. It was a rare evening when groupies weren't crowding the footpaths outside in the hope of glimpsing a rockstar and when you didn't bump into a John Cleese, a Bette Midler or a drunken executive from Channel Nine in the lift.

Shortly before the Sebel was knocked down for squillion-dollar condos, I had dinner with the Keatings and Janet Holmes à Court. Annita was the first to leave, then I had to head off to work at the wireless. This left Paul and Janet together for half an hour and, lo and behold, the very next day it was being reliably reported that they were having an affair. Very often such stories were peddled by restaurant staff. Given the clientele, Sebel waiters earned a few extra bob by phoning tidbits to the nudge-nudge, wink-wink gossip columns.

Another scandalous story from the Sebel. I'd had a late supper with a Minister of the Hawke Government. We met in the restaurant after I'd knocked off at 2UE. Terry, the high-camp maitre d', was characteristically attentive – though he made much more fuss of a hugely fat blonde lady, who turned out to be Mary of 'Peter, Paul and' fame.

The next day Terry rang to say, 'Your friend left his handbag under the table.'

My friend? Ah, yes, the Minister. But a handbag? I didn't recall him having one. Though for a brief moment it was considered kosher for straight men to carry little leather bags for their hankies and credit cards. So I asked Terry to open it.

'Perhaps there's ID inside.'

'I'll go and have a look.'

When he returned I asked, 'Any ID?'

'No.'

'Well, what was in it?'

'A pair of lady's knickers and a business card from A Touch of Class' – then Sydney's most notorious brothel.

A moment passed before I said, as calmly as possible, 'Yes, that'll be his.'

For almost a dozen years my columns in *The Australian* attacked the Howard Government. Though this went against the editorial grain, I was tolerated – perhaps I was a little useful. But for much of the time, criticising Howard seemed a lonely task and, consequently, I got angrier and angrier. Whilst there's no evidence my rantings had the slightest effect on the electorate, they did on Howard.

Just before his second federal election, the Prime Minister

was asked his principal reason for running. He answered that he wanted to 'prove something' to Robert Manne and Phillip Adams. Something, it seems, about his political legitimacy.

In fact, Howard inadvertently saved my job at the ABC by singling me out for special attention. When asked his major criticism of the public broadcaster, he famously enquired, 'Where's the right-wing Phillip Adams?' This phrase echoed and re-echoed around the building and was repeated by Jonathan Shier at Senate Estimates.

Then John Howard sent an emissary to visit me at home.

I am surprised – astonished – to get a phone call from the office of the Honourable Peter John McGauran MP in his role as Minister for, amongst other things, the Yarts. Could he visit me at home for a chat? On what? Policy matters.

So Peter, a quite amiable fellow, turns up and we talk about the film industry. Having spent decades on active service, I've made no public comment on industry matters for years but I'm happy enough to chat. My main problem is acute physical discomfort – months earlier I'd injured an arm, which is still so weakened that I can't even stir a cup of tea. The pain is constant and intense – and is immensely intensified when, suddenly, McGauran grabs it.

Both his hands embrace a wasted muscle and, as I all but pass out, he reveals the true reason for his visit. 'You've got to stop it!' he says with great intensity.

'Stop what?' I croak.

'Saying those awful things about the Prime Minister!'

He grips my arm even tighter while I tug feebly at his clenched fingers.

'You've no idea how much it upsets him!'

The effect on me and my arm is astonishing. It's as if I've been transported to Lourdes and experience a miracle. Though the withered arm is not restored, I'm suddenly aglow. I've no idea how much it upsets him? As the Minister takes his leave, I feel my time on earth has not been entirely wasted.

I had, for decades, preferred to fly on government-owned airlines. And that was easy because we had two government-owned airlines. Whilst right-wing friends flew Ansett, I preferred aircraft heavy with kangaroo insignia and two left wings. TAA and Qantas. And I habitually booked seat 1A to allow me to curl up in the corner and don an eye mask, thus encouraging sleep and discouraging conversations.

But during the Howard years I was, on a number of occasions, gazumped by another regular traveller, the very right-wing Janette Howard. Mrs Howard was allowed to accompany the Prime Minister on Australia's version of Air Force One – but if her husband was staying on in Brisbane, Adelaide or Perth, she was required to return on a scheduled airliner. And Qantas staff amused themselves by placing us together.

I cannot begin to describe Mrs Howard's facial expression whenever I'd (reluctantly) settle down beside her. 'Don't worry,' I'd say, as soothingly as possible, 'I'm going to sleep.' And I'd pull out my eye mask and pass out. And go on air that very night to announce that, yet again, I'd been sleeping with the Prime Minister's wife. Ah, the floods of protest that would assail ABC management and the board!

Midway through the Howard incumbency, the National Portrait Gallery commissioned a painting of the Prime Minister. In stark contrast to all its predecessors, it was a double portrait. He and Mrs H. standing side-by-side in a vividly painted and somewhat tropical setting. I understand that the board of that august institution had to modify the rules and regulations to allow this double-header to be included in the collection. There they stand, like an Antipodean version of Victoria and Albert or Napoleon and Josephine. Or, at the very least, Darby and Joan.

The pairing of John and Janette, this legendary double-act, became a part of Australian political mythology, their radiance eclipsing that of Gough and Margaret, Bill and Sonia, Malcolm and Tamie, Harold and Zara, Bob and Hazel, and Paul and Annita. So formidable was their alliance that the artist might have been tempted to paint a single body with two heads. My observation of Howard, over the years, was that he was one of the loneliest of men, with few friends inside or outside politics. But in Janette he had a friend indeed, his most loyal and trustworthy ally.

I was making this point once to someone who didn't like John Howard very much – a previous Liberal leader. 'At least they've got each other,' I said.

He looked at me with a mystified expression. 'What do you mean?'

'Well, at least John's got Janette and Janette's got John – it's one of the great political love stories.'

Let me emphasise that I was talking to someone who'd known the Howards forever, a very senior member of Howard's personal staff during his years in opposition and as federal Treasurer. He painted a different picture.

'When we'd arrive at the residence early in the morning – say seven-thirty for an eight o'clock start – we'd hear her yelling at him. Very loudly. And she'd only slightly reduce the volume when we knocked at the door. Sometimes he was so shaken by the experience that it took us all day to get him up and running. I reckon that's why he divided his time between the Lodge and Kirribilli House.'

I asked around the Press Gallery – could anyone confirm this dystopian version of the Howards' double-act? Nobody did, but I regard my source as reliable.

Where many a politician has voided his marriage vows, some with astonishing frequency, John Howard has always been a man of moral rectitude. Shameful, almost wishful rumours have arisen from time to time but, of course, all have been slanderous.

A senior member of the ALP and I used to amuse ourselves by imagining the high and mighty in sexual congress. And we agreed that John Howard would observe an enduring Australian tradition by not removing his socks. More importantly, he'd leave his spectacles in place. Which, we agreed, were unlikely to steam up.

As it became clear he was facing electoral disaster – and perhaps the loss of his own seat – Howard left Kirribilli House for the place of execution, the Wentworth Hotel. In 'Stop at Nothing', Annabel Crabb tells of a phone call the PM received as he crossed the Harbour Bridge. 'His recollection is that he answered it to find a jubilant Turnbull on the other end of the line. Turnbull was calling with the glad tidings that he had extended his margin in Wentworth. He also had some suggestions for Howard's speech.

'It is in remembering this conversation that Howard's amused tolerance with Turnbull is most in evidence.

'"He did ring me, yes, and the purpose of the call was to say something about himself."'

Nelson Eddy and Jeanette MacDonald, they of the silver screen, were billed as 'Americas singing sweethearts'. Yet their duets were dissonant when compared to the harmonies of Australian sweethearts Donald McDonald and his bride. Donald's Janet McDonald has been at his side throughout a long and diverse career, ranging from his managerial role in Harry M. Miller's doomed Computiket to his controversial chairmanship of the ABC.

And Don and Janet are the best friends of that other power couple, John and Janette. The Howards and the McDonalds are indivisible and, to many, the wives seem indistinguishable – remarkably alike in attitudes and appearance.

So much so that, on one historic occasion, Janet stood in for Janette – effectively playing her 'stunt double' in a dangerous scene.

With courage verging on defiance, John Howard fronted at the declaration of the polls for Bennelong in 2007. He'd not only lost government but, as you may recall, the seat. Where a lesser man would have stayed away, Howard braved the media pack and, with admirable gallantry, publicly congratulated his nemesis, Maxine McKew.

And as usual Janette was by his side. Only she wasn't. Perhaps she was busy that day, packing up at Kirribilli. Or perhaps this was the one event she couldn't face.

So Janet McDonald stood in for her. And nobody noticed.

Nine/eleven inevitably spawned conspiracy theories. One had the twin towers destroyed by Mossad, while another had the CIA and the FBI in an unusually efficient alliance. Also popular was the view that it was arranged by freelancers on instruction from the Oval Office.

Every day I was bombarded with conspiracies about 9/11. Most agree that the towers collapsed because of high explosives cunningly concealed in the building by a person or persons known to the conspiracy theorists. They are also of one mind in regard to any major role for al-Qaeda. Though some concede they might have helped Bush, Cheney and Rumsfeld in their great act of treason.

It is usually agreed that no jet hit the Pentagon. And that the jets that hit the Twin Towers were empty, piloted by remote control. Whereas some 9/11 sceptics believe that no jets hit the World Trade Center at all. Some correspondents solemnly inform me that the planes were illusions. Holograms.

I was moved, for the one and only time, to defend Bush. For him to have planned and executed the greatest act of treason in political history would have required the collaboration – and the continuing silence – of an army of operatives or irregulars. It would also have required a level of planning and managerial skill not on show in any of his Administration's other activities. We're talking about the gang who couldn't shoot straight in Iraq, one of the most stumbling and inept groups of dunderheads in political and military annals.

This earns me a death threat. I hear from a 9/11 nutter living in Melbourne that he and his coven of conspiracy theorists have met and decided that I must die. By denying the denialists, I've proved that I, too, am a part of the conspiracy. A stooge of Bush, Murdoch and the rest of them. He will, he advises me, sacrifice his own life in destroying mine. He will be a suicide bomber. He posts a letter to his mum on the net so that she will understand why he has to kill the both of us.

Having received a lot of death threats in the past, I've learned that officialdom isn't all that interested. Apparently, making death threats is fine unless you carry them out. 'Don't hesitate to get in touch if you're killed,' they always told me.

But this time they stir themselves and keep an eye on the bloke, promising to alert me if he's seen heading for the airport. At the time of writing these words, the death threat is still active and the death threatener is still under light surveillance.

Meanwhile, something nasty arrives in the mail. Not a dose of anthrax or some plastic explosives. A turd. Gift-wrapped in glad-wrap. I can only applaud the post office for its professionalism. It seems that half the CDs I get arrive in shards, but the turd is in mint condition.

Unsurprisingly, there is no return address. Nor is there any accompanying correspondence. I feel like demanding ballistic tests to see if it can be matched to the sphincter of a Gerard Henderson, Paddy McGuinness or Andrew Bolt. But apparently Australia isn't up to the technological standards of CSI Miami, Vegas or New York. The arsehole remains enigmatic.

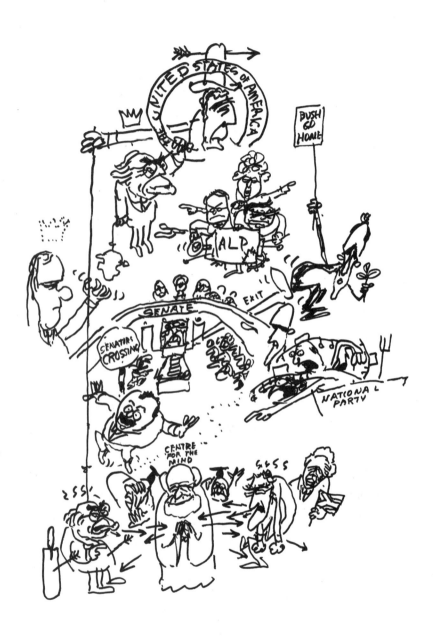

Senator John Faulkner visited the conservative electorate of Northcott, in New South Wales, to support the campaign of a Dr Therese McGee. They both spoke from the back of a ute, with the warm-up provided by someone Faulkner recalls as 'the quintessential bearded academic dressed in the traditional garb of the socially committed – duffle coat, sweater, corduroy trousers and sandals'.

When the ute drove into the most intensely conservative part of the electorate, the QBA (quintessential bearded academic) grabbed the mic and yelled, 'Workers and peasants of Beecroft, unite!'

And when they detoured by the toffy Beecroft Lawn Tennis Club, the QBA was even more inspirational – and less appropriate. 'Tennis players of Beecroft! Lay down your balls for Labor!'

✌

Soon after Laurie Ferguson became a federal MP, the Labor Government changed the laws on immigration.

'Suddenly, marriages involving people under eighteen years of age were not recognised for migration purposes,' Laurie told me. 'And I received a call from my secretary back in Sydney.

'A local party member's son had married a sixteen-year-old and wanted me to "fix" the problem. He was very agitated when advised that Australia had laws which MPs couldn't just override. He stormed out, swearing that he was voting Liberal and would bribe the Beirut Embassy anyway.

'Months later, he asked for an appointment. He came in with an older son and I recall him dramatically striking his forehead and saying, "I've just realised that your secretary didn't understand me when I came in about the marriage. She thought the girl was under eighteen. No, she was eighteen but the birth certificate was wrong and now we've fixed it."

'Naively, I telephoned Beirut with a supportive phone call. The immigration officer explained to me that they'd done bone scans of her wrists and the girl was definitely not eighteen years of age. I asked him about the birth certificate. He stated, "Over here you can easily get your birth certificate changed the first time. Changing it a second time does cause more problems, but these people have made a major mistake. They now have her born so early that it's before her parents were married – and that doesn't happen with Lebanese Maronites!"'

In 1999 Laurie went to Ireland with his wife and stayed with his father's cousin, Willie Burke.

'Willie had been chairman of the Galway County Council when

Paul Keating visited his ancestral village of Tynagh,' Laurie told me. 'Willie represented the most pro-capitalist of Ireland's political parties, the Progressive Democrats. After half an hour of what was only a foretaste of many hours of videos of the Keating visit, I indicated that even though Paul and I were in the same party, we were not exactly best friends. This was traceable to the then deep factionalism of New South Wales ALP politics.

'Next day we went to visit Willie's mother at the ancestral Burke homestead and farm from which my father's maternal line derived. Her maiden name was, of course, Keating.

'A few months later I was in a Chinese restaurant when Paul walked in with his kids. I told him that my father, Jack Ferguson, was very worried about the high level of intermarriage between the Keatings and the Burkes in that small corner of Galway. Keating thought it amusing enough to repeat the story to Laurie Brereton.'

Robbie Swan has represented Australia's porn industry for years. But before that he'd risked his reputation by being my producer at 2UE. Later we worked together on a political satire magazine called *Matilda*. Mungo MacCallum shared the office.

Robbie recalls that his first encounter with the National Farmers' Federation boss, Rick Farley, took place in the magazine's office.

'It was a freezing cold June evening. The office was about 100 metres from the Lodge and we were huddling around a single-bar radiator in the back room. I thought the idea of meeting an apologist for the National Party and a former cattlemen's union boss quite ridiculous. After all, we were a respectable character-assassination magazine. Not *Country Style* or *Hoofs and Horns*.

'When Rick walked in the door, the cliché was complete. Cuban-heeled boots, moleskin jeans and an R. M. Williams jacket. He shook my hand firmly, sat down and began engaging Mungo about the day's events in Parliament. Then, with a flourish, he pulled a packet from inside his coat and laid it down on the table. Now he had my interest.

'Like a chef rolling out puff pastry, he unveiled the largest marijuana head I'd ever seen. He broke off a large section and began laying a ten-paper joint. I was having difficulty reconciling this with anything vaguely reminiscent of Her Majesty's Opposition.

'He lit the monster spliff and inhaled like an old Rasta. I was also an old Rasta but Mungo declined. The more stoned I got, the more incredulous it all seemed. How could I have misjudged this bloke and the nation's primary producers for so long? Out there, between the tomatoes and the turnips, they were with us!'

Stuart Robert, the Liberal Member for Fadden, Queensland, won his seat at the November 2007 elections. He described to me his first Party Room meeting, in January 2008, when Brendan Nelson was elected Leader of the Opposition.

Senator Bill Heffernan stood to state – very loudly – that one of the problems with the 2007 campaign was the candidates. 'Next election we need a better bunch of candidates, rather than the bunch of fucking deadheads we had this time around.' There's a collective gasp and all eyes are on the seven new Liberals. Bill then modified the attack. 'Present company excluded, of course.'

The new MPs established the Liberal Class of 2007 and invite a luminary to their regular dinners, someone to impart his or her experience and knowledge. The first guest of honour was Peter

Costello. They call their group 'The Deadheads' and have invited Senator Heffernan to be Patron, and he regularly attends.

∽

Intrigued by Barnaby Joyce, I asked him for a few yarns. He responded with more of them than all his senatorial colleagues combined. James Joyce is famous for his 'stream of consciousness' approach to writing. Barnaby Joyce is comparably Joycean. For example, here he is having a drink with some 'fellow travellers at a Cloncurry motel'.

'I had probably had a couple too many rums and so had the person I was speaking to. I was advocating an inland rail to Darwin to give Mount Isa a port other than Townsville. He worked for the port authority of Townsville. The discussion had descended into insults and it was going very soon to be concluded "outside".

'In a brief moment of sanity, I begged leave of this enchanting company and went back to my room. I turned on the TV and there was an action movie on about a high-rise building fire. I was not in the mood for Bruce Willis or whoever the emerging hero was going to be, so I changed the channel. It was one of those late-night coincidences in low-rating periods where exactly the same movie was on, so I changed again. The same movie again – or was it the in-house movie jammed on all channels?

'Sitting on the edge of my bed in Cloncurry, a beer in my hand, I realised this was no movie and the world had just changed.'

Indeed it had. Almost all of us have a personal variation on Barnaby's story.

∽

'It all started when Bill O'Chee lost the Nationals Senate seat to One Nation,' Senator Joyce reminisces. 'Queensland had not warmed to three-piece suits and his proficiency in Olympic one-man bob-sledding. Bill's bobsled had run straight into Pauline Hanson and an electorate that had become highly sceptical of the party line as espoused by my party in Canberra. Our supporters were moving on because they did not believe we put them first. The Nationals had to change, not the electorate.

'The Nationals at that stage did not run on a joint ticket with the Liberals but stood in their own right. After two attempts at attaining a winnable position on the National Party Senate ticket, I fought a very tough pre-selection fight with the vice president of my party, Pam Stallman. After gathering the votes on a preselection campaign that had covered the state a number of times at my own expense, I, to the shock and dismay of the executive of the party, won, with James Baker coming second and Professor Stewart Gillies third. They pick the team they believe can work together, so when Pam came second in the vote for the top position they had a run-off vote for second and third, and the preselectors picked a team they believed could work with me.

'The campaign to win back the Senate seat was punctuated with all the wise political pundits not giving us a snowflake's chance of achieving a seat. I remember the pontificating in the media as to whether the last position would be won by the Greens, One Nation, the Democrats or even possibly the Liberals – all wrote the Nationals off as a bygone force. To add insult to injury, the Liberals ran a campaign targeting National seats with a photo of John Howard and the local National Party lower-house Member on the same National Party green banner colour, saying vote for my team but directing them to the Liberal Party Senate team. Many National

Party supporters, none the wiser till informed, turned up to the polling booths on election day with this same piece of literature.

'I spent about $40 000 of my own money campaigning, and with immense support from party faithfuls such as Lenore Johnson and others, we covered every two-horse town and community radio station we could find. Polling day was well supported by the pro-life lobby, who manned the booths where we could not muster National Party supporters, and the party faithful were, as usual, quite humbling in the support they gave the campaign where they could.

'The pundits were right, we did not win the twelfth spot but we went one better and won the eleventh. Of the approximately 325 000 votes that made the quota, only about eighty votes were preference flows from the Liberal party, with the quota being made up of National Party, the Fishing Party, DLP and One Nation votes. Quite an eclectic mix, and I never forgot that. I found it especially galling when Liberal supporters said I got in on their shirttails – anything but was the actual case.'

'The full sale of Telstra was the big issue at the end of the campaign,' Joyce continues. 'There were strong resolutions from the National Party state conference not to sell the final portion of the company because of the effects that would occur in regional Australia from a loss of control and interest from a fully privatised company. The election, however, had delivered the coalition a majority in both Houses and the Liberals had gone to the election stating they would fully privatise Telstra.

'With the announcement that the Nationals, represented by

me, had won a Senate seat, the phone in my accountancy practice literally rang off the hook. About sixty to eighty phone calls in two hours. My message spike was covered with my beleaguered staff's notes about calls from well-wishers and the media. One of those calls was from a bloke called John; my junior accountant had told him that I was busy and he would have to call back.

'As I made my way through my very new life as a Senator Elect, I found to my horror a note telling me to return a call from a John Howard. I gave my staff-member the mobile and went to ring him on the fixed line, but whilst I was doing that he rang back on the mobile and the same staff-member told him I was still busy.'

'Every media outlet asked me the same question,' Joyce writes. 'Would I vote for the sale of Telstra? I told them my party's position: no, I would not. My first swim in the big pool was going to be in the deep end with sharks and crocodiles.

'It was not long before the lobbying began in earnest. It was initially stated that we might get $600 million to assist in regional telecommunications if we agreed to the sale, and before talking to anyone I said no. Then my new leader, Mark Vaile, would announce some new "breakthrough" in the media and I would announce – also through the media – that I did not agree to it. It became apparent to my leader that he would have to get something that the Nationals in Queensland agreed to, if he was to have any hope of removing the pressure that was being placed on him by Howard.

'Bruce Scott, the Nationals' Member for Maranoa, decided that he would make himself a game-player by drafting a resolution that encapsulated a "breakthrough". I remember sitting in a management committee meeting. As Bruce wrote the resolution on a whiteboard, I got up and rubbed parts out and added parts in to try and make it as tough as possible – hopefully impossible.

'I had talked to Paul Budde, a telecommunications expert, and he had said we needed about $5 billion to deliver something for regional Australia but that this could be done in a public–private partnership, with only part of those funds being a subsidy from the Government. I had to find support internally in the party because I had been tagged a maverick and renegade. It looked like I was flying solo, and any support was quickly dissipating. Everywhere I went I found political operatives on missions to round me up, and I was very new at the game with no real trusted mentor to assist me.

'I remember the National Farmers' Federation dodging the question in a Senate Committee hearing as to whether we should sell Telstra because they had been asked to support the sale by Howard. I finally said to Peter Corish, the President of the NFF, "It is your decision. If you say do not sell, I won't."

'When put on the spot, he said – and this is in *Hansard* – "You have got a good deal! Sell!"

'The final nail in the coffin for me was that the resolution initiated by Bruce Scott and amended by me was passed by the Queensland Nationals' convention, to the sighs of relief of the ever-valiant Mark Vaile. I was now very much on my own – and isolated from my own party in my own state – if I blocked the sale. I did believe that Labor would sell it anyhow if they got the chance, only with nothing for regional Australia.

'In hindsight, I would never have voted for it, but I was very new at this game and that is why it was the first thing they threw at me.'

'Now life was a complete hell. It had started with coalition colleagues not giving me a seat to sit on in the joint party room, then Bill Heffernan was giving renditions to all of "last night I dreamt I was Barnaby", and the rest cannot be printed. It ended up in a very tense moment that was broken up by Peter Costello but then continued on in the Senate Chamber, where it was caught on camera. On the same day in the chamber I was both sworn at and sworn in. Now, after the Telstra vote, I was "Back-down Barney", and no matter how hard I tried I could not explain in one sentence – because that is all you get on the nightly news – what was going on.

'An ex-Labor Senator came and said g'day to me and gave me some very good advice. I genuinely believe it was one of the only pieces of sincere counsel I got. "You better find something you believe in and stick to it, or I can see you will destroy yourself."

'There was a vital piece of legislation that allowed big companies to become enormous and related to merger and acquisition powers. The National Association of Retail Grocers in Australia had come to St George in Queensland after reading my maiden speech, in which I spoke against the overcentralisation by Coles and Woolworths. They lobbied me to block this new merger and acquisition section, as it would put more pressure on independents by allowing more centralisation to the majors. The two men were Alan McKenzie and Associate Professor Frank Zumbo of the University of New South Wales School of Business. They finished their conversation with me at the Riverland Motor Inn Restaurant in St George with "Are you fair dinkum, because if you are you can make a big difference?" This was, for me, my time for some form of personal redemption.'

❧

'Crossing the floor in the Senate is not normal in the Australian political environment,' Senator Joyce writes. 'The last to do so in the coalition prior to 2005 was in 1992, and in the Labor Party it was Senator George Georges in 1986, and he was immediately expelled. Even the Greens have not split in their vote since 2004, and they are supposed to be the ones who rage against the established norm. Crossing the floor is held by some to be complete and utter deceit against the team; to others it is a terrifying epiphany for their electorate that you actually can vote as they desire rather than as you are told, however it will cost you a ministry or preselection. To others it is a perverse joy to watch someone do what you would love to do, but for the great personal cost. The Labor Party is completely intolerant of crossing the floor; Labor Senators are, for all intents and purposes, either Ministers or quite anonymous. They may as well have proxies, as their vote is a foregone conclusion.

'Anyway, I crossed the floor to omit a section on changes to the trade practices act on mergers and acquisitions. I had never contacted anyone in the Labor Party but they had got wind of it and had immediately collapsed the speakers' list – that is, they withdrew the speakers on the bill in order to quickly get to the vote, so as to avoid getting someone to speak to me.

'Andrew Murray from the Democrats I had taken into my confidence, as I saw him as an honest broker. We discussed the tactics and, as I walked into the chamber, he said, "This is it."

'Well, it was certainly "it" for me. Senator Ron Boswell said, "No, no, do you know what you are doing?" Jeannie Ferris, God rest her soul, said something far more abrupt. Kay Patterson screamed, "This is outrageous!". Another colleague said, "I hope you f-ing well die." For the next two years or so I had lunch and dinner by myself. Anyway, I believed what I was doing was right, and I was strongly prompted by the guilt that what I had done on Telstra, regardless of what I had achieved, was wrong.

'Strangely enough, after that, crossing the floor was not such a big issue, and maybe that is what party politics is terrified of elected members discovering. I strongly believe that seeing the Senate operate as it should, not as it has been manipulated, gives great strength to our true democratic checks and balances, which are the right of all citizens of this country and not the privileged property of the party machines.'

∽

John Forrest, the current federal Member for Mallee, recalls arriving at Parliament House in 1993.

'As I hadn't yet been allocated an office, I spent some of my first day wandering the corridors to familiarise myself with the place. Having found myself in need of ablution facilities, I asked a very well known Labor colleague, who was ambling down the corridor, "Do you know where the little boys' room is?"

'To this he replied, "You're new here, aren't you, son?"

'"Oh, yes," I answered.

'"Then let me give you your first lesson," he said. "There are no little boys here, only big boys."'

∽

'There's a well known showbiz adage that you shouldn't work with children or animals,' Peter Garrett says, 'but school visits are part of a pollie's beat. They have provided a number of the more amusing highlights of my political career.

'I am not often confused with other people, but I remember visiting a local primary school not long after nominating for the seat of Kingsford Smith to promote the education policy of the moment. As I walked through the corridor filled with excited children marvelling at the press pack and associated hangers-on, a young boy yelled, "Hey look, it's Michael Klim" – the Olympic swimmer.

'This was topped by a lovely anecdote passed on to me by the grandmother of a student at another of the schools in my electorate. I was scheduled to visit the school with a live native bilby (and handler) and talk to students about the plight of the threatened bilby. The young student excitedly told her family that the following day they were going to have a visit from a bilby and "a man from the Government". Grandma asked who the man from the Government was to be and the little girl replied, "Peter Rabbit."'

Nick Xenophon's senior policy and media advisor contributes the following:

'Three months after taking his place in the Senate, Nick was contacted by journalists about the fact he still hadn't met Prime Minister Kevin Rudd. This was despite the fact that Nick, along with the Greens and Family First, shared the balance of power in the Senate and might prove handy in getting some of the Government's legislation through.

'Adding insult to injury, certain members of the Canberra Press Gallery pointed out, the reportedly starstruck Prime Minister was about to make time to meet with Australian pop songstress Missy Higgins during a trip to New York.

'Unable to resist the chance for a dig, Nick first got stuck into the journalists who gathered for the traditional morning doorstop interview before each sitting day.

'"I don't think you guys appreciate the important role Missy Higgins plays in the Senate," Nick said with mock outrage to an initially confused and then bemused gathering of journalists.

'His office then put out a press release endorsing the PM's meeting and paying tribute to the contribution the singer had made to Australian culture. "If it was a choice between meeting me or Missy Higgins, I would choose Missy too," Nick said. "Missy rocks."

'The story was bouncing around talkback radio when word came through from New York that the PM wasn't meeting Higgins and had never intended to. The story was a furphy.

'Nick's office wrote, but never sent out, another release headed "Xenophon slams PM for snubbing Aussie icon".'

'Nick Xenophon bumped into Senator Bob Brown at Aussie's Café in Parliament House at the start of one sitting day and noticed Bob was under the weather. Bob had a cold that he couldn't shake.

'Nick, who has had more than his fair share of ill-health over the years, offered to contact his homeopath to have some tailor-made homeopathy solutions sent to Canberra to help get the Greens leader back on his feet.

'Bob politely declined, explaining he would rather leave the matter in the hands of practitioners of conventional medicine.

'"Don't tell me you're homeophobic!" Nick replied.'

Brendan Nelson reminds me of the death of the first Aboriginal elected to the Australian Parliament, the late Neville Bonner.

'I suggested to Slim Dusty and his wife, Joy, that his life would be inspiring material for a song. They then wrote "The Quiet Achiever", which was recorded for their 103rd album.

'When it was released in 2002 I was Australia's Education, Science and Training Minister. I had been in public life for approaching fifteen years. I went to the launch of the album and sat in the audience as Slim and the band rolled through the tracks on a new album. When they got to "The Quiet Achiever" Slim asked me up on stage.

'Needless to say, being able to sing along with Slim was a highlight, and the late-night news broadcast it to Slim's substantial audience.

'Next day I got off the plane in Wagga and the first man I met looked at me and said, with growing excitement, "I know you . . . You're . . . yeah, I know, you're the bloke that sings with Slim Dusty!"'

Bob Brown recalls the 1986 debate in Tasmania's House of Assembly on the Gray Liberal Government's enlightened bill to make all legislation gender-neutral.

'The bill got rid of the "he", "his" and "him", which had characterised all Acts since the House was set up in 1856.

'There was to be one exception. Section 122 of the Crimes Act prohibited homosexual acts, including sodomy, because, in the state where nature was routinely assaulted, such activity was "a crime against nature". In true Victorian style, the Government wanted this clause to remain male-specific. I expected the Labor Opposition to move to abolish Section 122 completely, but it did not.

'Suddenly, unprepared, it was up to me. I was about to get into one hell of a mess. Rattled, and knowing now that both Liberal and Labor would vote against removing Section 122, I moved to make it gender-neutral too, thinking this would never be accepted but would at least underscore the absurdity of permitting female–female sex while sentencing males, if caught *in flagrante delicto*, to twenty years in prison.

'But the House adopted my amendment unanimously. *Quelle horreur*! I felt the marrow in my bones melting. I went to my Hobart flat for a sleepless night.

'"Lesbians Outlawed!", or some such, screamed the front page of the Launceston *Examiner* the next morning. And, of course, the calls and letters of outrage began swamping my little office. Premier Gray had ensured I had no staff.

'My possible salvation was the Legislative Council. Notoriously conservative, this Upper House had been designed by Governor Eardley-Wilmot in 1856 to be a "watchdog" on the "excesses of democracy" in the Lower House. I phoned the least conservative of the councillors to plead that he oppose the amendment. In deference to Queen Victoria's sensitivities, even the British Parliament had not prohibited lesbian acts, I explained.

'"Well, no," he replied, "but the ban sounds reasonable to me."

'By now, national attention was focussing on the proposed ban on Tasmanian lesbian activity, heightened by the fact that I was the only open homosexual in Australian politics.

'Extraordinary as my predicament was, my saviour was no less unpredictable: Queensland's Premier Joh Bjelke-Petersen. On that same day, completely unrelated to the events in the Tasmanian Parliament, he, as a strident anti-homosexual, was asked if he would ban lesbian behaviour. Whether in deference to her late Majesty or not, I don't know, but he made it clear he would never back such a ban.

'Armed with this story from *The Courier-Mail*, I had a friend write to all nineteen Tasmanian councillors. The letter called on them to put the admirable Bjelke-Petersen's judgement ahead of the radical Bob Brown's.

'The Council promptly reversed my amendment to Section 122. I went to my bush home at Liffey and cried. But, my tortured soul saved, I slept like a saint.

'These days, I advise novice MPs to forego any temptation to outwit their Parliament with legislative impulse. "Do not move amendments unless you know the full consequences," I say – and say a silent thankyou to Sir Joh.'

Bob Brown remembers his eviction from Parliament in October 2003. Both Houses had been recalled for a joint sitting, to be addressed by George W. Bush and, the following day, by China's President Hu Jintao. All Senators were to crowd into the House of Reps, which Brown deemed inappropriate and unparliamentary. 'The House is a debating chamber for elected representatives of the Australian people,' he complained, arguing that 'the Parliament's Great Hall is the appropriate place for speeches by foreign dignitaries'.

'At 10.55 the bells rang,' Bob recalls, 'and MPs and Senators were required to stand as George Bush entered the Chamber. Laura Bush was in the gallery, along with US secret-service men with guns. John Howard and Simon Crean gave their short welcoming speeches.

'The black-robed Speaker of the House offered Bush the podium, which was adorned with the Australian coat of arms. Bush offered his scrambled eulogy to Howard, in which he claimed that the term "man of steel" was the Texan equivalent of the Australian "fair dinkum". Then came a long recounting of the invasion of Iraq and Saddam Hussein's weapons of mass destruction. My heart began pounding.

'Bush moved on to "freedom" and "democracy". It was now or never. As if on autopilot, I was on my feet. "Mr Bush," I said, "this is Australia. Respect our nation."

'The President stopped his speech.

'I pointed towards the Habibs and Stephen Price on either side of the chamber and continued: "Return our Australians from Guantanamo Bay."

'Objections from the assembled MPs were coming rapidly, especially from the Government side.

'Opposite, I ended with, "Respect the laws of the world and the world will respect you." I sat down, feeling strong and suddenly settled. Speaker Andrew ordered me to leave the Chamber.'

According to Nick Xenophon, there's no love lost between him and South Australian Premier Mike Rann. For years the two battled for the hearts, minds and attention of South Australians, and they often found themselves on opposing sides of an issue.

When Mike Rann claimed his Government was cracking down on problem gambling by reducing the state's poker machine numbers by a modest 3000, Nick was enraged.

A press release, clearly drafted in anger, took a swing at the

Premier with the following line: 'If Mr Rann is trumpeting this will make a big difference to problem gambling then I reckon he's suffering from a case of premature exultation.'

The relationship between the two went from bad to worse, where it remains to this day.

～

The Honourable David Hawker, federal Member for Wannon, recalls the final sitting day of the House of Representatives in 2005.

'The then Prime Minister, John Howard, was in the middle of paying tribute to his colleagues and family at the end of another political year . . . warning MPs that the grave affairs of state counted for nothing unless "when you depart this life you've got family around". At which point – *da-dum, da-dum, da-dum, da-diddly-dum da-dum* – up popped the hideous hat dance. Magnificently, somebody's mobile phone had sounded at the poignant moment.

'Everyone instinctively checked their pockets, but the owner of the rogue phone was – can you believe it – me. As Speaker, I normally booted people out for such transgressions, so I turned fourteen shades of violet before apologising for the interruption. It was my son, calling to tell me he'd passed his university exams.'

～

Gary Gray, the Labor Member for Brand in Western Australia, remembers his introduction to campaigning in the 1974 federal election in his home electorate of Grey in Whyalla.

'The Liberals had two candidates in Grey – a Liberal Movement and a Liberal Country League candidate. One day, one of them came knocking on our door. Dad let him in.

'I went into a complete tailspin. I could not believe that Dad had let a Liberal politician into our house. I was appalled. More than anything else, what would Gough think?

'Dad sat the Lib down and talked to him for a full twenty minutes, before coming into my bedroom to bring me out to shake the hand of this fine man, the Liberal candidate.

'I was turning mental cartwheels of anger, annoyance, and frustration that my dad had not only let a Liberal Party candidate in the house, he'd spoken to him for so long. Then he had asked me to talk to him and shake his hand.

'It got worse – Dad actually offered him a drink. My father is a Yorkshire man – Yorkshire men do not buy drinks, and they do not give away alcohol. But that day there was a Liberal Party candidate in the front room of our home, sitting on our sofa, sharing a scotch with my dad. I couldn't believe my eyes. I was making my plans to run away from home, when the conversation ended and the Lib was on his way out the door.

'Out the front, the Liberal candidate said, "If there is anything I can do for you, just let me know."

'Turning to his new friend, Dad said, "Well, there is," and proceeded to explain a problem with our Housing Trust – state housing in South Australia – home. "When it rains, water comes down the roof, hits the gutter, spills over it and forms a puddle on the path. If you step off the verandah you get your feet wet."

'The decoded message was that my father was always too lazy to clean out the gutters, but the Liberal candidate was a reasonably tall man and he reached up and pulled out a handful of leaves.

'"There's your problem," he said, as Dad looked on, amazed.

'"Well, I'd like to climb up there and clean that out," Dad said, "but with my back . . ."

'"No worries," said the candidate, reaching up again. In no time he'd cleaned the gutter out completely. That done, he shook Dad's hand and headed off up the street.

'I turned to my father and asked him, with all the self-control I could muster, how he could do that – invite this Liberal into our home and then make friends with him.

'Dad looked pleased and said, "He's just wasted an hour with us, and he's got alcohol on his breath and muck running down his sleeve. How many votes do you think he'll win today?"'

'I joined the Labor Party in May 1974,' Gary Gray writes. 'I did this after a bad experience on election night 1974, when, having worked for four weeks to get Laurie Wallace elected as the local Member, I wasn't allowed into the victory celebrations because I didn't have a Labor Party ticket. I think the real reason was that they had free beer in there, and they weren't about to give it away to just anyone.

'Until then, I had thought that being a member of the Labor Party was like supporting the North Adelaide Football Club. You wore the scarf, the beanie, you cheered the side, and so you belonged.

'And so I joined the ALP, partly so I wouldn't miss out on free beer in the future, but also to cement my commitment to the Labor Party.

'At my first meeting I was told that joining the Labor Party was about changing the world – it was about policy and protecting workers. As an example, the local branch president pointed to the fine white line on his schooner glass.

'"See this line?" he said. "That was a resolution the Whyalla Branch to the State Council recommended to State Conference as a platform amendment – it was passed, implemented by Don Dunstan and became law. So there, lad, that's how we make policy and protect people."'

⁓

'Crunching the numbers was something I learned about in 1979 . . . the hard way,' continues Gray. 'I was twenty-one years old. I had written to Des Corcoran, the then Labor Premier of South Australia, complaining about the behaviour of our local MP, one Max Brown, who had travelled the world on what in those days was a very rare affair – a political junket – a study tour on tourism.

'In his report, Max reflected, for instance, that in Barcelona he had been invited to attend a bullfight but had decided not to attend; he had cut himself shaving that morning and so, wrote Max, "I'd seen enough blood for one day and I decided to go shopping instead".

'In similar style, Max visited South America, the USA and then Britain, where he watched greyhound racing and returned home enthusiastically recommending that Whyalla become the global capital of greyhound racing . . . I already thought it was!

'Max's report was, in my opinion, truly appalling. So I wrote to the Premier and told him that Max was a disgrace and that he should resign.

'Within fourteen days, I had from Des Corcoran a letter saying that the Labor Party would deal with the matter, that he appreciated my letter and that he hoped the incident would not dampen my enthusiasm for the Labor Party.

'I was a bit surprised. This was the Premier of South Australia, and these were the days before word processors. A letter from the Premier was pretty impressive.

'The Whyalla sub-branch, I was sure, had sixty-six members; I had counted them many times. I went around the membership and I had thirty-four members who were prepared to back a no-confidence motion in Max Brown. The insurrection plot was working well.

'But there were a few things I didn't know, including the existence of a little-used clause in the rule book that gave affiliated union members rights in the sub-branch equal to those of party members, including votes. Neither did I know that Max's study tour was a reward for his pending early retirement.

'On the Friday night intended for the motion of no-confidence, two important things happened. First, a fellow called Chris Schacht – the State Secretary – arrived in town to put down the insurrection. Second, as we assembled for our sub-branch meeting, I spoke to people as they took their seats. I counted numbers, got to thirty-five, and was smugly confident. Thirty-five beat thirty-one, so I was sure to get my motion up – we had momentum.

'What I had not counted on was a fleet of minibuses arriving from BHP. They ferried shift workers from the wharf, the shipyard and the pellet plant, delivering 310 unionists to represent the unions' interests. What I also didn't know was that those interests were actually the interests of Frank Blevins, who later became the next Member for Whyalla and served the Parliament with distinction.

'The thing that cheered me up was that when the final vote was taken, my thirty-four plus one stuck with me – but unfortunately the numbers went 341 to thirty-five.

'Chris Schacht rose to his feet and said, "Well, what we witnessed this evening is a disgrace. I'll tell you what – a lot of people say a lot of things about Max Brown, but I'd much prefer to have a drink with Max than a drink with any of you," he said, pointing to me and my thirty-four mates.

'At that point I made my first interjection at a sub-branch meeting. "That's the trouble, Chris – Max will drink with anyone."

'In those days, Whyalla was a safe Labor seat and was the stronghold that gave the ALP the federal seat of Grey. Today, Whyalla is a marginal state seat and Grey is held by the Liberal Party.'

Warren Truss, the Minister for Trade from 2006 to 2007, wrote to me about chairing a meeting of the Cairns Group in Lahore, Pakistan, in 2007.

'The Cairns Group is made up of the Trade Ministers from nineteen countries and was established to lobby for freer and fairer trade in agriculture. It was an Australian initiative to create the Cairns group, which takes its name from the city where it first met.

'On arrival in Lahore, I could not help but notice the contrast between the peaceful beachside tranquillity of the first meeting site in Cairns and the intense security in Lahore.

'Lahore is close to the disputed India/Pakistan border, though these days the rivalry is better humoured and is played out in front of hundreds of spectators in a dramatic shouting match and the slamming of the border gates at six p.m. every day.

'But the Taliban trains nearby and other terrorist groups are active. In addition, the then President of Pakistan, General Pervez Musharraf, had recently dismissed the senior judiciary and there were protests on the streets and concerns the country may descend into civil unrest.

'Despite the security concerns, it was decided that the meeting should proceed, though the US Trade Representative, Susan Schwab, flew in and left the same day because of US concerns that it could become a target.

'The military presence was always obvious – heavily armed soldiers at the airport, around its perimeter and on the road to the city. The hotel was a fortress. A trip across the road to the Governor's Palace for the Welcome Reception took a full-scale army convoy. When our cars stopped in the traffic, soldiers poured out of the backs of the supporting military trucks, encircling our vehicles with their automatic weapons facing outwards.

'This was an important occasion for Pakistan, which went to great lengths to host the event lavishly and to raise the profile of such a meeting in their country. The highlight was a dinner and spectacular pageant held outdoors at the magnificent old Red Fort in central Lahore. Even though it was evening, the temperature was near forty degrees. The show was brilliant, with parades, camels and trains, all tracing the proud history of Pakistan.

'President Musharraf was present and he and I addressed the crowd from an elevated platform facing the pageant. Grandstands seating the invited guests were at each side. We then sat in armchairs on the platform to watch the spectacle with the Pakistani Trade Minister and the provincial governor by our side. The security and the military presence were very apparent.

'As the show began, I looked upwards to the turrets on the ancient fort and noticed that on every vantage point there were heavily armed sharpshooters with night-vision goggles overlooking the scene. For a moment I was comforted, but I soon realised that this level of protection was not there for me. And why was I sitting on this open stage alongside President Musharraf during a time when he was not rating very highly in the Pakistani Newspoll?

'I commented to the President that I hoped the sharpshooters were friendly. He reassured me, reminding me that he was not only President but also Commander of the Army. I needed no reminder, because this was the issue that had led to his dispute with the judiciary. Later he also confided that he was currently considering a list of promotions and so there were many people who had a strong interest in our remaining alive and secure.'

Rob Oakeshott, now the independent federal Member for Lyne but previously the Nationals' Member for Port Macquarie in the New South Wales Parliament, wrote me a long letter of anecdotes and observations, including the following.

'Nothing can describe the feeling of walking into a parliamentary chamber for the first time. After having gone through an election and convinced 50 000 people how great you are, it is with a sense of smallness that you enter a place with the history, the unique set of rules, and the real-life characters and personalities of politics.

'And it is not an exercise of just quietly walking in and taking a seat. No – the grandeur of being escorted in by two other MPs takes place, a bow to the Speaker takes place, a very public quivering voice of oath or allegiance takes place, a less-than-steady signature takes place, and then you're sent off to take your seat with an expectation by all that you won't be heard of for a year or two while you learn your unique and complex trade that is the Parliament. Oh, and whilst all this is going on – the sledging.

'I distinctly remember being less than three steps into the New South Wales Legislative Assembly when I heard "How sweet – fresh meat!" called out, followed by much laughter on all sides. I was only twenty-five at the time, the youngest MP in the place by what felt like a thousand years, and yes – I was intimidated.

'I was elected at a by-election, so all the usual pomp and ceremony of a first day in Parliament after a general election did not occur. Rather, the two sides – Bob Carr's Government and Peter Collins' Opposition – were in the heat of battle over a *Four Corners* program the night before that had alleged a link between media magnate Kerry Packer, the Sydney casino and the Labor Government of the time. Every question was targeting this topic and probing for different angles for a slip by the Premier.

'The Bear Pit was at its bearish best this particular day. Somewhat unerringly, in the heat of battle, every time the Premier got to his feet to speak, he was staring right at me. I was confused for some time, but then assumed it was a test. Whether he was trying to work me out, or testing the responses to his answers via my reactions, I was going to give him nothing! I thought to myself: I am an MP now and I am here to fight for my region!

'So I put a plan in place and stared back at Carr. This did not deflect his gaze, so I stepped it up a gear and leaned right forward to stare back at him. He continued his gaze. I then leaned back and stared at him. And I still couldn't shake his look. I couldn't work him out.

'After about ten minutes, I decided, *Australian Idol*-style, to judge the Premier with my body language. When he made a good point, I gave a slight nod of approval, and when he made a questionable point, I shook my head in dismay. All the while he continued to stare. And all the while I grew increasingly frantic. Was he going to mention me? Was he going to make some kind of allegation about me and the casino that I have never been to, or draw a link to the media mogul I had never met?

'I was stumped. It was only after about twenty minutes, when I'd taken a bit of a look around my new workspace, that it dawned on me: it was the television camera, stupid! It was right behind me. The Premier was directing his focus to that, and not at Mr "I'm Now in Parliament and I'm So Important!"

'So, for observers, you will notice next time you watch the New South Wales Parliament, that Premiers on the attack don't look across the chamber at the other side, they look to the top of the chamber to the one television camera that covers debate. And conversely, when uncomfortable and in trouble on an issue, a Premier, Minister, or any MP who is half-smart, leans on the lectern and looks towards the Speaker, as that gives the TV cameras nothing more than the back of a head for vision.

'It was not only my first day in Parliament, but also my first lesson on what really drives a modern-day politician.'

Also from Rob Oakeshott is the following story.

'At twenty-five and asked to enter politics, it was easy to say "Yes" as I had nothing to lose – no money, no wife, no kids, no house. Just a couch and a surfboard and a very old car. So into the service I went, into a campaign I went, and – through the efforts of many and the kind support of voters – I was elected.

'At the time I was dating an extremely exotic, beautiful, charming nineteen-year-old called Sara-Jane. Sara-Jane was part South Sea Islander, part Aboriginal and part Scottish. But when asked where she came from in that nervous, "you know what I mean, why is your skin darker than mine" kind of way, she would reply, "Port Macquarie," and then enjoy watching people try to re-ask what they really meant. She was a beauty!

'At the same time a highly controversial – for some – piece of legislation was passing through the Parliament, a proposal that the age of consent for homosexual sex be uniform with that for heterosexual sex, i.e. sixteen years of age. This had many MPs in twists and turns, in particular on the conservative side of the fence. Through some rather stretched logic, they had decided to vote against the bill and try to argue for two different ages of consent – sixteen years old for heterosexual sex, and eighteen years old for homosexual sex.

'The only problem was that one conservative MP had an openly gay son, whom he loved dearly, and he was therefore not at all comfortable with the position that the conservatives were taking. He therefore took it upon himself to go around to each MP and ask them was it okay if he "abstained" and didn't vote. "Of course," I said. This answer was a visible relief to a man caught between his political party and his family.

'So, with this context, I walked into my first party meeting, completely intrigued by how it all worked. Unfortunately, one of the opening comments from one of the grandfathers of the Parliament was one that still makes me angry to this day. This conservative, western New South Wales MP rocked back in his chair, took a deep breath and, to the sniggering of some of his cling-on colleagues, said, "What's happening to this once great party? It's getting overrun by blacks and poofters."

'I am now a happily independent MP and have left party meetings a long way behind. I am now also happily married to the girl in question, Sara-Jane, by whom I have been absolutely captured since she was nineteen. I am sure the MP with the gay son is still close to him, or at least I sincerely hope so. And as for the bloke who made that comment – who knows and who cares what happened to that rancid old racist homophobe, who taught me that there comes a time in a young man's political life one has to start saying "No" as much as they say "Yes".'

Woody Allen lookalike and all-round genius Professor Allan Snyder cajoles the Australian National University and the University of Sydney into co-sponsoring his Centre for the Mind, where he plans to continue his researches into almost every aspect of human consciousness. One of the most admired and awarded scientists of recent times, Allan is voraciously interested in the genius, the prodigy, the autistic, the bipolar and the way the brain functions. His work – and his personality – attracts international attention, admirers and antagonists. And his Centre for the Mind conferences will attract the best and brightest – Oliver Sacks or, on the occasion of this story, Nelson Mandela.

I'd managed to get some foundation funding from Lachlan Murdoch, who'd joined the original board, along with an odd collection of luminaries including Baz Luhrmann. Allan's chutzpah in approaching celebrities to participate in CFM events paid off. Scientists and savants found themselves rubbing shoulders, even noses, with the likes of Richard Branson. But Mandela? Even I was amazed that Allan had managed that.

I was chairman of the advisory board and, cross my heart, John Howard was our patron. In the run-up to the great day, I was told that the sequence of events in the Great Hall of Sydney University would be as follows. The Vice-Chancellor would introduce me. I would introduce the Prime Minister. And the Prime Minister would introduce Nelson Mandela. Afterwards, I would move the vote of thanks.

The thought of introducing John Howard was unpalatable – to Howard as well as me. But the VC insisted. This was the proper protocol, and all I had to do was be respectful of Howard's high office and say a few welcoming words. But as the hour approached I felt increasingly mutinous.

Then I was saved by the bell. Actually, by a phone call. It was from someone in Howard's office, who said, 'You don't really want to introduce the Prime Minister, do you?'

'Of course I don't.'

'No, it would be a bit hypocritical.'

'Not as hypocritical as Howard introducing Mandela.'

I would remind the reader that John was a supporter of apartheid and opposed the international sanctions against South Africa. Whilst his predecessor Fraser was held in high regard throughout Africa, Howard most certainly wasn't. But clearly he couldn't lose the opportunity of publicly identifying with the sainted Nelson.

So there was a change of arrangements. The Vice-Chancellor would introduce Allan, who would introduce Howard, who would introduce Mandela, then I'd move the vote of thanks. A major relief to at least two of us.

As we milled around in the quadrangle, Howard and I managed a curt nod. But then came trouble. Easter Island arrived. Malcolm muscled his way through the crowd to Mandela. During an affable exchange, Fraser spotted Howard and immediately started bellowing out a loud attack.

He told the story of a group of Vietnam refugees – people who'd been close to the Australian Embassy – and his determination to grant them asylum. He'd phoned Whitlam and got the nod – the whole thing was to be done quietly, below the radar. Cabinet had also agreed – with one exception. 'Yes, *him*!' Fraser bellowed, as he pointed at Howard, who was standing a few feet away. He condemned Howard's response as deeply bigoted and disgraceful. It was, by any measure, an increasingly ugly and interesting scene.

The VC begged me to do something about it. Could I keep Fraser at a safe distance until the ceremony started? So I cajoled Malcolm into joining me in an anteroom for a cup of tea. It was just off the Great Hall and was set up with urns of boiling water and a choice of teabags. I suggested that Malcolm sit down whilst I'd make us both a cuppa. He chose English Breakfast and a very low armchair by a majestic marble mantel. And he proceeded to sit.

With his buttocks targeting the upholstery, Malcolm's speed of descent increased and, alarmingly, he hit his head on the mantelpiece. For a couple of seconds he was knocked out.

Oh my God! They'd made me responsible for a Prime Minister and I'd killed him! Even worse, I'd killed the *wrong* Prime Minister!

Malcolm came to, slightly puzzled but unconscious that he'd been unconscious.

A few minutes later, I steered him back into the Great Hall. As promised, the VC introduced Howard, who introduced Mandela – fulsome in his praise, as though there'd never been a moment's disagreement on South African policy. Mandela spoke magnificently. I was able to sink the slipper into Howard during my vote of thanks and the day ended without further incident.

Mandela knew that something had been going on but didn't let it fuss him. As for Howard's words, he was clearly used to having international dignitaries rewrite history with regard to their roles during the apartheid years. But he did take me aside to ask me, in a low whisper, 'How's Paul Keating getting on?'

For decades the National Trust kept itself busy protecting teetering buildings. In 1997 it decided to turn its attention to tottering people. It conducted a poll to identify 100 'living treasures' – which had the almost immediate effect of killing many of them off. Perhaps it was the excitement, but Arthur Boyd, Ruth Cracknell, Elizabeth Jolley, Edward 'Ted' Matthews (the last Gallipoli survivor), Morris West, R. M. Williams, 'Mum' Shirl Smith, Mavis Taylor, Sir Roden Cutler, Charles Perkins, Betty Archdale, Slim Dusty, Alan Walker, Nancy Bird Walton, Judith Wright, Mark Oliphant and Dons Bradman, Horne and Dunstan were soon 'dead treasures'. And I wasn't feeling all that well.

(The poppies scythed by the Reaper have since been replaced by newly elected treasures – as was Marcus Einfeld.)

I wasn't alone in being shocked by my inclusion, which critics saw as confirming a left-wing bias in the listing. Yet John Howard made the cut – as did every living PM, with the odd exception of Robert Lee Hawke. Certainly a majority of the treasures, living or not, weren't on Howard's side in the culture wars. Discounting the apolitical ranks of the cricketers, racehorse trainers and sundry sportspeople, all the usual criminals had been rounded up by the National Trust's voters – the 'black armband' historian Henry Reynolds, Indigenous leaders such as Lowitja O'Donoghue, Faith

Bandler, the Dodson brothers and Noel Pearson (then one of 'us'), and sundry subversives including Barry Jones, Bob Brown, Judy Davis, Germaine Greer, Tim (not Peter) Costello, Mikes Leunig and Kirby, David Williamson, Tom Uren, Julian Burnside, Jack Mundey and, perhaps worst of all, the Bolshevik Bill Deane. Amongst Howard's few friends? Geoff Blainey.

Yet with customary courage Howard agreed to officiate at the official launch at the Sydney Town Hall. Come to think of it – how could he refuse? Boycott a ceremony in which he himself was honoured? Along with his greatest hero, the Don? Thus, we were bussed to that great municipal mausoleum and arranged in an embarrassed cluster beneath its soaring organ pipes, and the PM did his best with a bad lot. Somehow he managed to imply his distaste for the majority without actually saying anything rude. Although I fully expected him to do a Bob Ellis and climax his part in the proceedings by chundering on the stage.

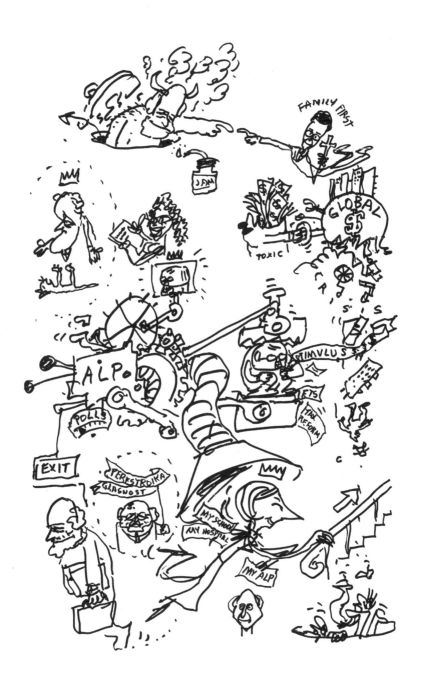

I feel the need to confess. Amongst my more improbable friends is a Pentecostal minister with one of those vast suburban congregations. On any Sunday he packs into his Perth version of California's Crystal Cathedral a greater congregation than any of the once-unassailable brand-name faiths. We argue the toss from time to time, me deploring the tendency of our booming Pentecostalism to follow the US example and align itself with the hard right.

There, the 'Republican base' that backed Reagan and, more recently, George W. Bush supports wars, rejects public-health reform, denies evolution and is maniacally hostile to gays. Here, the latter problem – homophobia – remains central to the Church of England, particularly in the Sydney diocese. By and large, Australia's Pentecostal industry is profoundly conservative across the range of social issues.

To my surprise, my friend invited me to make these points to an annual conference of Australia's Pentecostalists. Describing myself as 'a mangy lion in a den of Christians', I was surprised by their cordiality. I'd expected signs of the cross and cries of 'Unclean, unclean!'

I expressed relief that the Australian Pentecostalists hadn't formed themselves into a religious phalanx like their American counterparts. 'Because if you did,' I said, 'you'd be unstoppable.' I urged them to remember that there are other models for religious engagement in politics – and talked of the profound importance of Christians in everything from destroying slavery to, more recently, aiding the civil-rights movement in the Deep South.

I left after polite applause. A few weeks later, my friend phoned with some shocking news. 'We talked afterwards about what you'd said – about how powerful we'd be if we got ourselves politically organised. So a group of us went into a room and decided to do just that.'

And Family First was born.

∽

Barry Jones and wife Rachel have shifted to Brunswick. I visit them as they tackle the detritus left by a convoy of removalist vans. While Rachel looks glumly at all the boxes of books, Barry hangs a few of his favourite pictures – including a marvellous collection of bark paintings.

My attention is caught by a framed photograph. Large and lurid, it shows the innermost folds of a red rose in a confronting close-up. It is a truly erotic image, verging on the pornographic. Perhaps it deserves a designation of its own. Floragraphic?

I blush and avert my gaze as Barry points to the signature of the proud photographer. Imagine my astonishment when I see that these looming labia were on the receiving end of a zoom lens owned by none other than Malcolm Fraser. With the rage of 1975 no longer maintained, Barry and Malcolm have become close friends. Despite celebrating his eightieth birthday the ex-PM has not lost his legendary lust for life.

∽

Not long after 9/11, the ABC began to increase security – to the point that it now takes me seven swipes of my ABC pass to get from the street into my studio – seven booms, iron gates and Checkpoint Charlies. Nonetheless, vulnerabilities remain – particularly in the mailroom, where there's a serious shortage of X-ray machines and sniffer dogs.

One day, whilst I'm far away from Harris Street, a parcel arrives that at first causes concern and then consternation. Addressed to me, it has, according to the mailroom, 'strange writing on it' that 'might be Arabic'. So the entire building is evacuated. The ABC's umpteen radio studios are switched to autopilot and the TV studios are abandoned. The children are awoken in the crèche, the staff ushered from the cafeteria, the executives from the twelfth floor. Producers, presenters, techos and bleary-eyed babies are mustered into Harris Street and a call is made to the Bomb Squad.

You might have expected an armour-plated truck to arrive and disgorge blokes wearing visors and protective suits. You might have expected a robot to approach the package and prod it, or even fill it with bullets. Instead, a Falcon turns up from the local police station and a couple of young cops wander in, grab the parcel and toss it into the back seat. They manoeuvre the Falcon through the crowd and neither they nor my parcel are ever seen again. There's something wonderfully Australian about the response, an almost inspiring blend of the anti-dramatic and incompetent.

Slowly, the ABC's troops return to their tasks, the kids to the crèche, the programming to normal. When I finally hear about the parcel, I'm pretty sure I know what it was. At that time of the year I always got three or four jars of marmalade from a listener in Melbourne, Simonette Guest. She'd have a friend in Sydney drop the jars off.

I don't think the parcel was jammed with explosives. I think it was jammed with jam.

But I shouldn't mock the ABC's security measures – or the official response to a threat. When Simonette had her marmalade delivered the previous year – to my home in Paddington – my long-term PA, Sandra Blood, tossed the parcel into the swimming pool.

Sandra was not of a nervous disposition. Instead, she made other people nervous. Unfussed by phone calls, no matter how lunatic or lofty the caller, she tended to give the wider world short shrift. Yet there was something about Simonette's package that had aroused her suspicions. So she simply tossed the parcel into the swimming pool. Where it promptly sank. We fished it out a few days later and the marmalade was delicious.

Protective of her employer, Sandra has provided me with more security than was enjoyed by anyone and everyone at the national broadcaster. After thirty years, she is still the world's fastest typist and we remain a double-act. Indeed, she's transcribing these tapes as fast as I dictate them.

Writing about Gough towards the end of his term of office, Malcolm Turnbull suggested that the then Prime Minister had 'fallen into the classic trap of the egomaniac . . . This childish business of putting his leadership on the line every time he doesn't get his own way is straight out of the Elysée Palace in the days of de Gaulle.'

My story of Whitlam's hissy fit in the 1960s reads like Malcolm's views in 1974. Yet Malcolm will forget the lesson of history and have hissy fits of his own.

Malcolm's political career has had, at last count, at least as many lives as a cat. And this raises the issue that Malcolm's life has been haunted by feline references. 'Even a dead cat bounces,' critics observed when he failed to show resilience in the polls.

In a 1991 profile, I described Malcolm Turnbull as a 'pussycat'. This reference was taken by the legal and political cognoscenti as a veiled reference to perhaps the most contentious episode in his career. A story known simply as 'The Cat', it involved Fiona Watson, an uncommonly attractive young woman who was Senator 'Diamond' Jim McClelland's stepdaughter. In the late 1970s she was the focus of Turnbull's amorous attentions but, perhaps exhausted by his emotional intensity, she stopped answering his knocks on the door of her Double Bay terrace.

Then, according to legend, Malcolm started writing letters to Fiona's cat, trying to recruit it as an ambassador. These days, Malcolm says he can't remember the correspondence but one letter has been produced by the editor of *Justinian*, Richard Ackland. Hastily scrawled, it is by any measure a passionate epistle.

Shortly after the cat had failed as a go-between, the creature was found dead on the perimeter of Fiona's property. Malcolm argued that it was probably run over, but Fiona believed it was strangled. Rumours swept Sydney about this feline fatality. There were allegations that the cat's strangler was, yes, Malcolm Turnbull.

The best account of the fable can be found in 'Stop at Nothing', Annabel Crabb's *Quarterly Essay* on 'The life and adventures of Malcolm Turnbull'. Apart from Malcolm's protestations of innocence, it tells of a 'small gossip item by Richard Ackland' in *The National Times* in 1981. Ackland, 'in the course of some observations about Mr Turnbull's candidacy for Liberal preselection in the federal seat of Wentworth, wondered archly what the cat-lovers would make of him'. Turnbull's writ was in the mail and 'the matter was settled in Mr Turnbull's favour, with modest damages'.

Crabb writes that, 'several years later, another Fairfax columnist was incautious enough to add the sobriquet "Cat Strangler" to Turnbull's name in print. Again, Turnbull intervened quickly and secured a settlement.'

(Note: 'I did not strangle my girlfriend's cat' will become one of those long-lingering lines like 'I did not have sex with that woman' or 'Yes, but I didn't inhale'.)

Conrad Black, currently incarcerated, tells another version of the story in his autobiography, *A Life in Progress*. Annabel Crabb explains how the book's Australian edition 'restrains itself to the prim recollection that "Malcolm's fugues were notorious, such as the time (as a young single man) he allegedly punctuated an altercation with a friend by disposing of her cat"'. However, the US version has him 'sneaking into her home late at night and putting her kitten into the freezer, transforming a frisky pet into a well-preserved corpse'.

References to 'the cat' have popped up from time to time – in an Alan Ramsey column and various political cartoons. Crabb concludes, '"The cat" became a piece of eastern-suburban folklore. When Turnbull represented Packer through the "Goanna" affair, the satirist Max Gillies appeared as Packer, with a stocking pulled over his head; his routine contained a reference to cats, which would have made sense only to the initiated.'

Crabb provides a postscript. 'The episode earned Turnbull . . . the lasting hatred of the late Jim McClelland, who in 1991 had this to say of Turnbull: "He's a turd. He's easy to loathe, he's a shit, he'd devour anyone for breakfast, he's on the make, he's cynical, he's offensively smug." Turnbull shrugged at the time that McClelland was "a bitter old man . . . I'm very sorry that many years of excessive consumption of alcohol and professional disappointment have reduced what was once a sharp wit to nothing better than gutter abuse."'

Another story from Annabel Crabb on Malcolm Turnbull, this time in his role as patron of the arts. The family had approved Lewis Miller to paint their portraits. 'Miller chose to depict Malcolm and Lucy in close profile on two separate canvases, in the style of Piero della Francesca's famous diptych *The Duke and Duchess of Urbino* . . . The portraits of the children – Alexander and Daisy – are still in the Turnbulls' Point Piper home, but the parents are nowhere to be seen: Malcolm and Lucy didn't like the paintings much. Miller recalls that he commenced another portrait of Turnbull for the Archibald Prize in 1995, but Turnbull – shown the work in progress – did not like it and withdrew his coopera-tion. Turnbull registered his disapproval with the art dealer Ray Hughes . . . "That artist of yours is no good. He's made me look like a fat, greedy bastard."

'"Well, Malcolm," rasped Hughes in delighted reply. "You must remember that he is a *realist* painter."'

There are various stories about Malcolm flirting with Labor pre-selection. What is not in dispute is that in the mid-1990s Malcolm was discussing the possibility with Labor heavies, including Paul Keating. Malcolm insists that the process was 'initiated by Keating' and that he declined. Graham Richardson will have none of it – the discussions were initiated by Turnbull. Richardson has written that Turnbull asked for a Senate spot in 1993 but lost enthusiasm when Richardson reminded him of the demands of a grassroots ALP membership. Whatever the truth of it, the politically ambidextrous Turnbull turned up as a Liberal.

Mikhail Gorbachev was a fixer. A fixer who broke things. I'm sure he had no intention of wrecking the Soviet. Just wanted to plaster over some of the cracks. But, like Joshua tumbling the walls of Jericho, Gorby undermined the Kremlin's.

Years later, I spent a weekend with Gorbachev. The scene was a conference in Brisbane, where I was charmed by his affability and his Hawke-like physicality. Like Bob, Gorby is a back-patter, a hugger, a bloke who invaded your personal space. And at all times he was accompanied by a loyal translator, a drab, sad little bloke who could stand beside Gorby at a lectern yet effectively disappear. He reminded me of Woody Allen's Zelig.

When the three of us sat down to record a long interview, I noticed that this man was translating his boss's answers before Gorbachev had finished giving them. Sometimes it seemed that he could translate Gorbachev before Gorbachev had spoken a word. Well, he'd heard it all before. He'd been subtitling Mikhail for decades. At one point I suggested to Gorbachev that we go outside for a cup of coffee or to puff on some Balkan Sobranies and leave the interpreter to do the interview solo.

Not that Zelig was having much fun. While he translated to-and-fro, he stared glumly at his wristwatch, a cheap Russian number, as though willing the time to pass. He'd shared a remarkable adventure with Gorbachev, up to and including the Reykjavik negotiations with Reagan. But nothing Gorbachev could say had the power to surprise him. He was, as they say, bored shitless.

Things might have improved for him had the woman pounding on Gorbachev's hotel door at three a.m. been admitted. Gorby's room was on the same floor as mine and his nocturnal visitor was a woman who'd shared a Nobel Peace Prize.

'Mikhail! Mikhail! Let me in!' she was imploring, completely ignoring the 'Do Not Disturb' sign dangling from the doorknob.

I imagined poor Mikhail cowering on the other side of the door. And had he admitted her, would he have called on his translator? To interpret requests made during the act of congress? Slower! Faster!

Bob and Blanche throw a dinner party at the Hawkes' nest. Its purpose is another attempt by Bob to repair relations with Paul. Joining Paul and his partner are Miriam Margolyes and hers, and a French aristocrat with his long-term girlfriend.

Bob is at his most charming, effusive in his praise of Paul – 'We were the best team in Australian political history' – and the initial stiffness melts, to the point where each of the guests is asked to do a performance piece. These take the forms of songs or anecdotes and, as the evening progresses, the atmosphere becomes warm to the point of being cloying.

So much so that the French count makes a particularly dramatic contribution to the entertainment. 'This is such a wonderful evening, and I am so deeply moved that I now wish to propose marriage to my lovely companion.' Which, to her delight and astonishment, he proceeds to do.

After her joyous acceptance, it is Margolyes' turn to do a turn and she announces that she will, as might be expected, do a bit from her one-woman show on Charles Dickens. But first she said, 'I agree that it has been a marvellous evening. And I must admit I didn't know why I was invited. But the invitation I got was intriguing: "There'll be two Australian Prime Ministers and a French cunt". Needless to say, I was curious.'

Not to be confused with the double portrait of John and Janette Howard in the National Portrait Gallery, the double portrait of John and me that appears on the cover of this book first appeared on the cover of *The Spectator* – the Australian edition, edited by Tom Switzer. Whereas the John and Janette duet in the NPG shows a couple besotted with each other – though one of the stories in this book calls that into question – the image of John and me is somewhat ambiguous. We seem to be dancing. Or are we wrestling? Either way, I seem to be making sexual advances that John is reluctant to receive.

I thought it odd of Tom to invite me into his conservative organ. But we go back a while. For a few years he edited the opinion pages of *The Australian*, where I, like a lonely little petunia in an onion patch, surrounded by right-wing ranters, used every inch of available space, week after week, to give Howard some curry. Tom joked about my contributions as being 'contrarian' and defended me against the rage of readers. John Howard, it would emerge, was unamused – as another story in this book shows. When it was all over for Howard, Tom resigned from *The Australian* and, in due course, would be on the A-list of candidates fighting for preselection in Bennelong, Howard's old seat. In between, he worked as an aide-de-camp to Howard's unsuccessful successor, Brendan Nelson.

I wrote any number of columns urging Turnbull upon the Libs, seeing him as a sort of Arnie Schwarzenegger figure for the Libs. Progressive in social and climate-change policies, very much on the left of the Libs, another independently wealthy strongman who came to politics a self-made celebrity, Malcolm was just the bloke to give the Opposition a bit of a rev-up. Such were my enthusiasms for Turnbull that, on the day he finally turfed Brendan, Tom told me they'd rushed round Parliament saying, 'You can't vote for Turnbull – he's Adams' candidate.' For once, my support was not a kiss of death – although the graceful, grateful, handwritten note from Malcolm thanking me for my efforts went missing in the mail.

Having just missed out on Bennelong, Tom got the *Spectator* gig and suggested a one-off contribution. Which, to my surprise, he put on the front page, along with the double portrait under discussion. 'I never thought I would miss Howard,' said the banner.

As we both expected, there was an indignant response from *Spectator* readers, both local and expat. And one of the responses came from the man I was seen embracing. As Tom tells it, Donald McDonald was sitting in a leather chair at the Australia Club awaiting the arrival of his best friend. To fill the time, he was leafing through one of the club's copies of *The Spectator*. When Howard arrived, he looked at the cover with repugnance. 'I'm cancelling my subscription.'

I asked Tom to pass on my assurances that I would never sully *The Spectator*'s innards, let alone its cover, again. But now the cartoon has taken on special meaning for me. And I thank both Tom Switzer and cartoonist David Follett for letting me borrow it.

∽

As Beazley was flagging in the polls in 2003, Mark Latham was waiting in the wings and got himself a column in the *Daily Telegraph*. Far from repudiating Beazley on the refugee issue, he decided to exploit voter bigotry by urging an even tougher line. And instead of using his column to attack Howard, he used it to attack his own party's bleeding hearts, which he saw as eroding Labor's energies. With a wink and a nod to the ALP's proud involvement in the White Australia Policy, he unilaterally suggested the reintroduction of capital punishment.

And he attacked me in column after column. We'd never actually met but glared at each other across airport lounges. Instead of attacking Labor's enemies – Tim Blair, Andrew Bolt, Gerard Henderson and the ultra-con pundits who devote their lives to vilifying the Labor Party – Latham singled out the one columnist who had, for decades, unswervingly supported it. This provided additional proof of Latham's lack of political acuity, strategic skills and leadership qualities.

I was reminded of what Barry Jones said to me just before John Howard's 'dark victory' at the height of his carefully choreographed refugee crisis, when the PM tried to sink the SIEVs as surely as Thatcher had the *General Belgrano*. With Australia capitulating to Hansonism, Jones, the President of the ALP at the time, said, 'The voter has a wonderful choice at the elections. If they want 100 per cent of One Nation, they vote One Nation. If they want 95 per cent of One Nation, they vote for the Nats. If they want 90 per cent of One Nation, they vote for Howard. And if they want 70 per cent of One Nation, they vote for Beazley.'

I was appalled at the prospect of Kim Beazley retaining or regaining the ALP leadership in 2003, let alone handing over to Mark Latham. While the former was affectionately known as 'the Bomber', he'd christened the latter 'the Bomb', insisting that the only question was whether he'd explode before, during or after being anointed by Caucus. I was fascinated by a bloke from Queensland whom I'd interviewed on *Late Night Live* – Kevin Rudd – and we began talking. He'd come around for cups of tea and conspiratorial chats, but he couldn't get the numbers for an initial challenge and was subsequently swept aside by Latham, who, as expected, exploded at all points – before, during and after winning the leadership.

One of Rudd's principal problems in winning friends and influencing Caucus was that he's a passionate God-botherer, albeit one of sophisticated theological tastes. I found myself suggesting that his Christian conservativism might in fact be an advantage in campaigning against Howard. Either way, the religious issue had to be tackled directly.

I talked to Sally Warhaft, editor of the increasingly influential journal *The Monthly*, and she invited Kevin to contribute an essay. He recycled some thoughts on Dietrich Bonhoeffer, the heroic German theologian whose opposition to Nazism led to his martyrdom.

Convincing myself that Rudd's admiration of Bonhoeffer would surely 'kick in' if and when Australia was confronted with another refugee crisis, I was happy for him to be a true believer in both the cross on Golgotha and the light on the hill. (His Beazley-like behaviour over refugees from Sri Lanka and Afghanistan would have disappointed Bonhoeffer. It certainly disappointed me.)

The article caused a furore among the ALP's doubting Thomases, but the net effect was that Kevin's religiosity was dealt with and subsided as a concern – in much the same way as Blanche D'Alpuget's biography of Bob had made his sexual appetites less of an issue.

For Kev, it was a case of third time lucky – his next lunge at the leadership was successful. And within minutes he had started to demolish the mythology of Howard's political genius and unassailability. Soon, to our mutual astonishment, Rudd was in the Lodge. The campaign strategy was simplicity itself. Though derided as 'Howard Lite', Rudd reassured an anxious electorate. And God had answered this atheist's prayers.

Prior to his ascension, one of my columns urging Kev on Caucus provokes a strange response. I get emails telling me that Rudd is very rude and naughty – that he's up to all sorts of sexual hanky-panky. When I tell him about the accusations the next time he visits, he's understandably alarmed. Who's sending them? Will they get out?

Not via me, I assure him, as I've already deleted them. And I try to calm him by pointing out that the emails accuse him of a smorgasbord of sexual appetites that would usually be regarded as belonging to entirely different diets. You can hardly be both a Hannibal Lecter and a vegan.

Paul Keating has spoken movingly about the ANZAC – 'not of sweeping military victories so much as triumphs against the odds, of courage and ingenuity in adversity'. This on the occasion of the reburial of an 'unknown soldier' in Canberra. Previously, we'd made do with Britain's unknown soldier, but it had been deemed necessary, as part of a cultural maturation process, to have one of our own. So, on the eleventh of the eleventh in 1993, Keating talked of 'a legend of free and independent spirits whose discipline derived less from military formalities and customs than from the bonds of mateship and the demands of necessity'.

But he has no time for the focus on Gallipoli. Launching Graham Freudenberg's *Churchill and Australia* in 2008, he spoke again of his admiration for Winston ('I was attracted to him for his braveness, sense of adventure, compulsion and moral clarity,' he had earlier written, adding that Churchill's example had inspired him to enter politics), while deploring the nationalist mythology about Gallipoli that early historians and John Howard had peddled.

'The truth is that Gallipoli was shocking for us. Dragged into service by an Imperial government in an ill-conceived and poorly executed campaign, we were cut to ribbons and dispatched – and none of it in the defence of Australia . . . For these reasons, I've never been to Gallipoli and never will.'

Within minutes of Keating's speech, Kevin Rudd publicly attacked him – distancing himself from his predecessor's words in a surge of trad patriotism. Given that Paul had spent a lot of time giving Rudd backstage advice on a raft of issues, he was shocked by the PM's press release, which was clearly aimed at placating the shock-jocks. Rudd had no need to buy into a brawl involving a few tabloid editorials and shock-jock rants.

'Why would he do that?' said the puzzled, angered voice on the phone to me.

'Because he resents owing you so much,' was my reply.

It was part of a familiar pattern between Keating and Rudd – of mild tantrums and warm reconciliations. When Rudd was seeking the leadership I spent a lot of time as a go-between – turning Keating from a sceptic to a qualified supporter. But spats continued – and continue – to occur.

David Marr's *Quarterly Essay* on Kev tells of a 'roast and fundraiser' for Rudd when he was a 38-year-old contender for the seat of Griffith. Kim Beazley, then the Deputy Prime Minister and destined to become a roadblock in Kev's brilliant career, told the crowd a little story about Gareth Evans. When Evans had been elected to the Senate, his colleagues at Melbourne Uni gave him a set of luggage – 'to carry his ego to Canberra'. Beazley added, 'You might like to think about that, Kevin.'

At the 20/20 summit, with Rudd the ringleader to a thousand performing intellects, I tick him off about failing to front at John Button's funeral. When that great tribal gathering was taking place in Melbourne, Kevin was taking flowers and chockies to Cate Blanchett in hospital. Her tiny baby took precedence over the tiny Labor hero – you couldn't miss the huge colour photograph on the front page of *The Sydney Morning Herald*.

While Kevin tried to make amends by starring at Button's wake, the damage was done. It was further proof that he was too easily seduced by celebrity – something I saw as evidence of his essential innocence. Kev was thrilled to be seen with marquee names – as when he'd detoured to visit Russell Crowe on his first trip to the USA as PM.

Cate and Hugh Jackman co-starred at the 20/20 summit – and I'd seen both the Jackmans and the Kidmans at a Kirribilli dinner, where Thérèse told me there'd be many such gatherings in the future. 'We want to have another Camelot!' she'd murmured excitedly. I reminded her that Jackie had invited poets, philosophers and other lofty creatures to break bread, not just movie stars. Having become stars themselves, the Rudds ceased to be starstruck when the stars struck back, criticising the PM over his criticisms of the Henson photos.

Over the years Kevin often rang the farm on a Saturday afternoon and we'd have meandering chats. On the weekend before the 2009 budget he phoned three, four times over the morning. Rory would answer, say that I was somewhere on the place and promise to give me a message. But she forgot – just as she sometimes forgot who 'Kevin' was. I drove to Sydney that afternoon and there were three messages from the PM, increasingly querulous, on the machine.

Following standard procedure, I sent a text message to his mobile: 'Back in Paddo . . . ring anytime.' Clearly something was urgent, so I expected a quick response – but it didn't come until midnight, just after I'd DND'd the phones.

It was a week later, after the usual budget brawlings, that he phoned again.

'Sorry about that,' I said. 'What was the problem?'

There was no problem, he insisted, just felt like a yarn. Not believing him, I went through an agenda. Something to do with *The Monthly* fracas – over the sacking of Sally Warhaft? (I'd introduced them when he was after the leadership and I'd recommended he write something on his religious beliefs to reassure Caucus that he didn't wrestle rattlesnakes or talk in tongues other than English or Mandarin.) No, it wasn't that.

Was it the ABC? Film policy? No and no. Just a chat. So we had one, but when I was finally saying goodbye he said, 'Oh, there is one thing.'

It all came out in a rush. He felt Chris Mitchell was waging a personal war on him, through *The Australian*'s news stories and editorials. We'd discussed this earlier but now it was deeply disturbing him. I repeated what I'd said on earlier occasions – there was nothing I could do about it. It was between him, Rupert and Chris.

'But there is something you can do about it – you can resign! You can resign to protest the paper's editorial line.'

I declined to make myself a blood (or Rudd) sacrifice. 'And why worry about it?' I said. 'If Obama can endure *Fox News* you can cop the *Oz*.'

A little later Mitchell and Rudd seemed to have kissed and made up. Kevin became the paper's Australian of the Year.

Long before he gained the leadership, Rudd showed none of the self-doubt of Beazley. Like many, if not most, of his predecessors – Hawke, Keating, Whitlam and Fraser – he believed he was born to rule. When it came to the big job, he had the same sense of entitlement. Beazley infuriated him by not stepping aside in his favour after the fall of Simon Crean. Rudd couldn't get sufficient numbers to mount a plausible challenge to Latham – who openly detested him. And when Latham lurched off the stage to rewrite his diary, Rudd faced Beazley again and, as the last man standing, took the prize.

But for all the intensity of his beliefs – in Christianity, in Bonhoeffer and in himself – Rudd was still astonished when he won a far bigger election. The weekend before he presided over his first Parliament in Canberra, he invited me to Kirribilli House for a victory dinner. When I arrived he was standing in the doorway. Neither of us said anything. We just burst into laughter.

The laughter at Kirribilli's door ended abruptly on Wednesday 23 June 2010.

For decades the ALP had protested the Kerr coup, ululating over the vice-regal regime change that had deposed Whitlam. The Dismissal? Thirty-five years on, factional thugs now dismiss leaders at their whim. In cowardly conspiracies. First, a rapid succession of New South Wales premiers. Now a Labor prime minister.

For once, and only once, I found myself in agreement with Tony Abbott. Removing a PM from office is a job properly left to the electorate. It's what elections are for. Now the faceless men were trundling the tumbrels and the guillotine was working shifts.

For over a month my membership renewal had been languishing on my desk. Paying to remain in the New South Wales branch seemed problematic. The assassination of Rudd made a final decision all too easy. After fifty years of membership, through thick and thin – mainly thin – I resigned.

Not that this caused the party a moment's concern. Seems only yesterday that Mark Latham was writing in his *Daily Telly* column that 'there's no room for Phillip Adams in the modern ALP'. (Our argument, incidentally, had been over refugees. Mark wanted to be tougher than Ruddock.)

We're told that everyone loathed Rudd. Apparently, I'm one of the very few who didn't. Indeed, I'd become fond of him. We'd met on *Late Night Live* in May 2001 and soon after became friends. Despite our religious differences, and my ideological views that put me closer to Gillard, I admired Kevin's intelligence and, yes, his ambition. To put that in context, ambition was sadly lacking in Beazley, the Al Gore of Australian politics, and that as much as anything had doomed his prospects.

So in column after column I had pushed the idea of Rudd as Labor leader. It took three leadership challenges until, through sheer persistence, he got up. And because of his conservatism he beat Howard, as I'd always thought he would. Just as he'd have beaten Abbott.

In his agonising farewell speech, Rudd referred to various staffers and colleagues as 'good humans'. Well, Rudd is a very good human. Few in the upper echelons of politics have comparable idealism. Even fewer share his intelligence and ethics. Of course he has flaws – but they're offset by his essential decency. And to see him cut down by thugs without decency, working in darkness, disgusted me.

Like Keneally in New South Wales, Gillard took power courtesy of some very unpleasant people. I'm assured that the new Premier is another decent human being. I barely know Julia Gillard but accept that she was coerced (or seduced) into her challenge. Yet I was deeply troubled throughout her cleverly calibrated victory speech. First of all, some victory! Secondly, she justified the coup by talking of a government losing its way. But it was *her* way! As Deputy PM and heir apparent, she had more than a casting vote in the 'Gang of Four'. And at least one of the most calamitous decisions was hers: the dumping of the Emissions Trading Scheme. Rudd resisted, she insisted.

If there were problems in Rudd's office, if the ministry felt disregarded, if – as many Labor heavies were telling me – this was 'the worst-run government since Whitlam', then Gillard should have led Cabinet to carpet Rudd, to sort things out, rather than leading them in a coup. Instead of being grown-ups they were gutless wonders. It seems they were as timid with Rudd as coalition MPs had been with Howard.

Rudd and I talked often, and oft argued. About, for example, the climate-change policy he'd finally dump, on the insistence of Gillard. (Odd how Gillard would justify her coup against Rudd by citing policies she herself had driven.) But while I disagreed with some of the tactics, nothing would have persuaded me to support a move against the leader who'd defeated Howard, who'd made that superb 'Sorry' speech and who'd handled the GFC with such skill. The right to dismiss a PM belongs to all of us at an election, not to a drunken Governor-General or factional bullies drunk with power.

On Thursday it was over. Rudd goes, so I go too. Seems the lethal Latham was right.

We'd planned 'Rudd's first interview since the coup' for the previous week. Kevin knew I'd totally opposed the coup and had resigned from the ALP in protest, so *Late Night Live* would offer a safe haven.

That afternoon, while doodling on his pad, trying to formulate a few words he could say about Gillard in good conscience, Kevin felt a blinding pain. A clear case of getting the Gillards in the gizzards. Following the recent re-enactment of Act One of *Julius Caesar* – all those blades in the back – it was off to hospital for the kindest cut of all. The surgeon's scalpel.

(A word on Shakespeare's play. As Kevin pointed out, the Bard deals with the Ides of March concisely. 'Et tu, Brute . . .' then Caesar falls. The bulk of the drama concerns the grisly ends of the conspirators.)

We spoke again while Kevin was emerging from the fug of anaesthesia – when he literally didn't know what day it was, mistaking Wednesday for Tuesday. I told him my first question would concern his ghostly, ghastly appearance at Gillard's launch, which, oddly, was scheduled for the campaign's final hours. This prospect fascinated me. Still does.

(Let's recall the context. Keating had been hidden from public sight at the Latham launch, being smuggled through a side door while Whitlam and Hawke made the grandest of entries. Whereas on his big night Rudd had given Paul an honoured place in the proceedings. There they were – Whitlam, Hawke and Keating, side by side, burying their hatchets for the evening. And make no mistake – there was little love lost between any of them. Keating and Hawke despise each other and neither has much respect for Gough, seeing the Whitlam Government as a farce. Gough, in return, views the younger men as lacking his historical and heroic stature.)

Rudd now seemed in an impossible position. If he appeared, he'd have to be the most enthusiastic member of Gillard's audience, smiling like a Cheshire and clapping like thunder – for the cameras would never leave him. It would be as painful as gall-bladder surgery without anaesthesia. Rudd would be the story, not Gillard.

But if Kev stayed in bed, he'd be branded a traitor.

I knew Gough wouldn't make it this time. The old dear was too poorly. And that Paul wouldn't be seen dead in the same hall with Hawke in the light of the Bob 'n' Blanche book and their TV biopic. So Julia was going to be a bit short of ex-PMs on her big night. To make matters worse for Rudd, he'd have to stand beside Hawke, who had been amongst the first to publicly call for his assassination.

That night Rudd handled my question with grace, candour and some humour. He took the same approach to all the rest of them. Yes, he'd been through hell, and so had the family. Everyone knew that. But no, he couldn't let his life be destroyed by bitterness. Whatever conflicts he'd he had with Gillard were naught to his issues with Abbott.

Kevin's voice was initially frail, gaining strength to bucket both David Marr and Robert Manne for what he regarded as their unhelpful pop-psychology in *Quarterly Essay* and *The Monthly*. But it was back at full roar as he contemplated Abbott stealing government. So, yes, he was ready to help Gillard. To fight the good fight anywhere and everywhere. Even to attend the launch.

Things went crazy at the ABC while we were talking. While my producers tapped out a transcript on the trot, the rest of the media were monitoring and sampling. Every journalist in the land was demanding access and there a tumult of twittering. Even before the program had ended, you could sense that Gillard and Co. were capitulating – that they'd be begging Rudd to return. Very sensible of them. The response from listeners was unprecedented. In hundreds of emails they were welcoming, demanding him back. Where the conspirators had looked callous but competent, now they looked like clowns.

The only question Kevin ducked: would he have beaten Abbott? I put to him what I'd argued for weeks – that having despatched Howard, Nelson and Turnbull, he'd have trounced Abbott as well. The poll figures used to justify the coup? I reminded the listeners that Howard's had been far worse towards the end of his first term. Modesty and strategy forbade a response. Listeners were left with the impression of someone bruised, battered, bloodied but unbowed.

What no one knew was that, after we talked, Kevin had collapsed. A lot had hinged on what he said that night.

The first time I'd interviewed Rudd on *LNL*, eight years earlier, I'd said, 'Let's keep an eye on him – he's got a big future in politics.'

He's got a big future in politics. I repeated those same words after the interview, and the response showed that my audience overwhelmingly agreed. Certainly, Rudd's return made Abbott's future in politics more problematic. He now had to campaign against not one but *two* prime ministers. Gillard/Rudd. Or was it Rudd/Gillard?

A listener made a good suggestion. Why not keep them both on as joint PMs? Rudd could have the Lodge, Gillard Kirribilli.

The issue of the official launch remained, yes, an issue. How would Team Gillard handle it? I predicted Rudd would get a standing ovation when he walked into the hall. What would that signify for Gillard? Surely she had only one option: to lead the applause. And Hawke would have to join in.

Only Paul Keating wouldn't have a problem. He had a diary clash.

Finally, my favourite story – as told by Greg Crafter, who these days heads the Dunstan Foundation. The characters? My lifelong friend Clyde Holding and his then missus, the earthy and honest Margaret.

'I was visiting the island of Rhodes in the late 1980s,' writes Crafter. 'It was a formal visit and one evening we were being entertained at dinner by the island's dignitaries. During the meal, a woman tapped me on the shoulder and asked if I remembered her. I didn't. With polite prompting she told me that she was "Clyde Holding's first wife".

'Margaret told the story of Clyde spending many hours on a very hot summer day with a large number of protesters outside Pentridge Prison calling for Ronald Ryan's reprieve. The Bolte Government had made an example of Ryan as a key component of its gung-ho approach to criminal justice in that state, and Ryan was to hang. The police were present in large numbers and delighted in making many arrests.

'As the day wore on, a police sergeant arrived along with other members of the constabulary leading police dogs. Clyde loudly exclaimed, "They've brought the fucking dogs in now!" The sergeant heard Clyde and immediately arrested him for abusive language, and in the ensuing scuffle other charges evolved. Clyde was chucked into a paddy wagon, where, in the company of other protesters and several drunks who had been in the vehicle for hours, he was taken to the city watchhouse, charged and bailed.

'Some months later there was a trial in the Magistrates' Court in Melbourne, Clyde having pleaded not guilty. From memory, Frank Galbally QC appeared for Clyde. The arresting sergeant was grilled by Galbally for hours, and at the end of his evidence he didn't know up from down. Holding was duly acquitted. Margaret sat through the trial and endured all the unpleasant publicity that surrounded it.

'Some months later again, Clyde was elected Leader of the Opposition in Victoria. One of the first official functions Clyde and Margaret attended was a dinner party at Government House. They were duly driven to the dinner in their official car. Margaret was sitting in the rear seat.

'As they approached the entrance to Government House, a police officer opened the gates and stood to attention, saluting the vehicle and its occupants as it entered the vice-regal domain. Who should be the police officer at the gate? None other than the arresting sergeant from the Pentridge Prison protest.

'Margaret quickly wound down the window of the car, politely leaned out of the window and said, with great joy, "Where's your fucking dog tonight, Sergeant?"'

Normally, an author's dedication begins a book. In this case, right here seems more appropriate. I dedicate these pages to Aurora Alexandra Newell Adams, who turned eighteen while I was writing them, campaigned for the Greens and voted for the first time in August 2010. She's now at Edinburgh University studying politics, picking up where I leave off . . .

Index of names